# GEM
# MAGIC

# GEM

# MAGIC

*crystals and gemstones for love, luck, and power*

*Brenda Knight*

**FAIR WINDS**
PRESS
GLOUCESTER, MASSACHUSETTS

First published in the USA in 2004 by
Fair Winds Press
33 Commercial Street
Gloucester, MA 01930

Library of Congress Cataloging-in-Publication Data

Knight, Brenda, 1958-
  Gem magic : crystals and gemstones for love, luck, and power / Brenda Knight.
     p. cm.
  ISBN 1-59233-024-X
1. Precious stones—Psychic aspects. 2. Crystals—Psychic aspects. I. Title.
BF1442.P74K65 2004
133'.2548—dc22

10 9 8 7 6 5 4 3 2 1

Cover design by Carole Goodman, Blue Anchor Design
Book design by Laura Herrmann Design

Printed and bound in Canada

*The information in this book is for educational purposes only and is not
intended to replace the advice of a licensed medical professional.*

In honor of all the teachers of my heart, most especially Robert Kent Leffler, from whom I learn wisdom each and every day.

*Oh, Son of Summer. Every Season Is Yours*
—"Birthday Solstice," June 21, 2003

Brightest blessings and a major attitude of gratitude to the Goddess of Generosity, Kat Sanborn, who shared knowledge, great incense, and good cheer at all times. Blessed be.

Many thanks to Kat's partner in love and life, the late Tim Maroney, who loaned me invaluable books from his incomparable library for research for this book before he passed on July 3, 2003. Tim, your brilliance still shines.

*We must be still and still moving into another intensity. . . .*
—T. S. Eliot, "East Coker"

# CONTENTS

# ACKNOWLEDGMENTS

First and foremost, my thanks go to my family, especially my mother, Helen, and Aunt Edith, who mentored me from my rock-tumbling days till now. They taught me to seek knowledge and to share the love of learning.

Thanks also to my special friends the Wild Siders, Lillian Crist and Sheryl Schlocker, who brought me food, astrological updates, and support as I wrote this tome. I could not have done it without you! And eternal thanks to Anna Amato, researcher and wordsmith extraordinaire!

My agent par excellence, June Rifkin Clark, fellow Piscean and nurturer of the creative impulse, I send you my gratitude.

I extend my appreciation to all the fair folk of Fair Winds who believed in this book and made it beautiful, especially my editor, Paula Munier, who saw the jewel in the rough in the first manuscript and had brilliant instincts and advice about how to polish and set this crystalline book, and the wonderful assistant editor, Janelle Randazza, who keeps her eye on the prize and also sees the magic of gems growing.

Finally, my thinking around the magic of stones, crystals, and gems was enriched by Barbara Walker, with whom I have had the honor of working, by activist Starhawk, by priestess Z Budapest, by scholar Luisah Teish, and by the great magician, gemologist, and author Scott Cunningham.

# INTRODUCTION

Welcome to the wonderful world of gems and crystals! Together we are going to explore this magical realm, and you will discover which stones are exactly right for you. Certain stones will bring love into your life; other gems will heal your body and give you a sense of well-being. Still others will help you get to the depth of your personal creativity.

This book is organized in such a way that in the first section you can learn how, when, and why to apply gem magic in your daily life. The second section of the book is a veritable encyclopedia of gem lore and explains the specific qualities of each and every stone and crystal. Throughout, I have included tips and tidbits for easy, instant ways to make magic with minerals. You will also learn how to make your own jewelry and create "power tools" of your own—wands, amulets, pendulums, and all manner of magic makers.

Gems only enhance your life, and I have long enjoyed the benefits. Gems have gotten me through heartache and helped me find new and true love. Gems have aided me in finding work and achieving abundance and prosperity in my life. Crystals have also seen me through a life-threatening health crisis and caused my doctors, friends, and family to remark upon my seemingly miraculous healing. Was it a miracle? Perhaps. Was it magic? Most definitely! Gem magic, to be sure.

*Part One*

# WORKING WITH GEMSTONES

*Chapter One*

# THE GLORIES AND WONDERS OF GEMS, CRYSTALS, AND STONES

As a child, I loved the varied colors of rocks and crystals and asked for a rock tumbler for Christmas. Remember those? Soon, I was tumbling away and making some very low-budget jewelry for my sisters, my mother, and myself. Everyone raved about the shiny, smooth stones glued (rather sloppily, as I recall) onto crude bracelets, rings, and necklaces. A February baby, I felt pleased that my own birthstone, amethyst, was so readily available, and my sister Martha was a bit disappointed that I couldn't provide her with her April birthstone—diamond! My mother loved her peridot gifts and still wears a little leaf onto which I glued a tiny, polished peridot.

During my childhood, I also loved walking around in the woods. Pretty rocks with unusual shapes or colorations would grab my eye, and I would come back home from my Thoreau-esque wanderings with pockets filled. At the age of 11, I read J. R. R. Tolkien's *The Hobbit* and then immediately dived into *The Lord of the Rings*. Now, Tolkien knew of the power of gems and has contributed greatly to their legend and lore. I remember reading enviously about the Dwarves' glittering caves and treasure troves. For me, it was no mystery that the One Ring was evil, because it was a plain band inscribed with the language of Mordor in Elvish script and with no stones at all, while the rings of the heroic Elrond, Gandalf, Galadriel, and Aragorn all featured beautiful stones. Stones and gems were good and had the power to help vanquish evil? Yep, this I could completely understand. Even in the lavish and terrifically entertaining film version of this epic trilogy, stones have a starring role. I think I especially enjoy when Gandalf claps a big quartz crystal onto his wizard's staff to light the way when he and the rest of the Fellowship enter into the Mines of Moria, a real den of iniquity as evidenced by the most unwholesome Balrog! Oh, and then there are the lovely and mysterious *palantir*, or seeing stones, which I can only guess are super-powered crystal balls! What delight—I love that millions and millions of people, quite literally, are being introduced to the supremacy of stones in this way. I must confess, as well, that when the line of *The Lord of the Rings* jewelry came out, I couldn't resist ordering a Dwarven Ring of Power, with a lovely blue stone.

Growing up, I was very lucky. I had an Aunt Edith, my Uncle Edison's second wife, who mentored me. She took me under her wing and taught me many things. I make much mention of Aunt Edith in my *Witch's Brew, Good Spells* series and how I owe her for my small wisdom. She taught me about plants and their uses in cooking and healing. She taught me about trees and how to identify each one by bark and leaf. She taught me about the stars in the sky and the constellations, a perfect preparation for the astrology we delved into later on. And, thankfully, she taught me about rocks and gems and crystals.

She and Uncle Edison traveled a lot around the country; I remembered thinking they had a much more glamorous and adventurous life than we did. Now, I know that their children had grown and left home, and they simply had the luxury of time to drive around North America. But, drive they did, and everywhere they went they collected a rock, which they proudly displayed at their home. Naturally, Aunt Edith had a story about each rock. I remember some striated slate from Yellowstone and some granite from Devils Tower, but things really got interesting for me when they went to South Carolina and came back with some rather cloudy yet very green emeralds. I couldn't get over the fact that you could just dig in the earth or clamber up a mountain and crack off chunks of precious stones! To me, this rockhounding sounded too good to be true, and I was ready to hop in their station wagon and go on the road with them, hammer in hand, to prospect. Since I hadn't even made it to junior high school yet, I was not allowed to accompany my beloved Aunt Edith and Uncle Edison, but I knew we would have gotten along famously and come back with untold riches.

Aunt Edith mentored me in ways I only now appreciate. When I showed a special interest in something, she encouraged me to read and explore and study as much as I could. She immediately saw that I was crystal crazy, and she oh so patiently led me through the mysteries of rocks, crystals, and gems.

From her, I learned that even the earliest humans made use of the unique properties of crystals. For example, amber, one of my absolute favorite gems, was probably the first stone used as ornamentation, when people of the Stone Age discovered the rock-hard resin deposits. We have seen roughly rounded beads used for necklaces, belts, and pouches. Archaeologists and anthropologists have found many sites in which precious amber was buried with the tools and remains of shamans, medicine men, and rulers. Since the beginning days of mankind, this stone has been thought to have healing properties, a belief that stays with us to this day. Frequently, various gems were made into powder and taken orally as medicine. Obsidian was another early stone used for decoration, as we can see from deposits dating back to the Neolithic Age. And, the first humans polished the shiny surface of jet and used it for mirrors to see not only the present but also the future.

But the Egyptians were perhaps the people most conscious of the power of crystals, using them even in the cornerstones of the Great Pyramids. They used gems as objects of protection, power, wisdom, and love for both the living and the dead. A very important part of their burial ritual made use of the proper stones lapis lazuli, obsidian, turquoise, quartz, and carnelian by placing them inside the burial chamber. Each stone had a specific purpose necessary for the fulfillment of the ritual; for example, carnelian had the power to transport the souls of the dead to the other side. People traveled far and wide throughout the ancient world to obtain these precious, pretty rocks.

## THE POWER OF GEMS

Where do gemstones get their power? They all have a crystalline structure that can collect, store, and release electromagnetic energy, similar to the way today's commonplace battery does.

Scientists and engineers have discovered through experimentation that a crystal will accumulate and concentrate the energy of any given energy field in close proximity. Further, they've discovered that if a crystal is squeezed, energy from within the crystal is released. Light can also be released during the compression of a crystal. While the expansion is infinitesimal, electrons are emitted and are then reabsorbed by the crystal, thus producing energy. Schoolchildren discover this by rubbing or heating crystals and feeling a marked static charge. This is known as the piezoelectric effect. Anyone who doubts the power of this effect need only be told that it is one of the causes of earthquakes!

Quartz is the crystal most often used today in both scientific and spiritual realms. It is, perhaps, the most prevalent of all gemstones and can be found on every land mass on Earth. Common quartz was used in the world's first radio broadcasts and enabled the chips that propelled the computer revolution. It stands to reason that quartz was the first crystal to be synthesized by manufacture. Today, man-made crystals are in vast usage in our watches, computers, and other electronic devices.

Quartz is composed of silicon and oxygen, the same basic minerals that make up this planet. Silicon dioxide ($SiO_2$), the building block responsible for the geologic makeup of the earth, is also inside us, which may explain why there is a natural attraction between our bodies and crystals.

## Tips 'n' Tricks

### DREAM CRYSTALS

Thomas Edison carried quartz crystals with him at all times and called the stones his dream crystals. He believed they inspired his ideas and inventions. Literary legends George Sand and William Butler Yeats also relied on crystals to help spark their considerable creativity.

Data has also been gathered to show the effectiveness of quartz in certain healing techniques, such as chakra therapy, acupressure, and light-ray therapy, as we will discuss in depth later. But the simplest way to promote healing with crystal is to wear a stone.

Quartz can take the form of great hexagonal stones or of crystals so small that only a microscope can see them. Quartz can appear in clusters or singly. It can also appear in every hue of the rainbow. The gorgeous and varied hues of quartz come from electrostatic energy, which now can be altered through technology. I, however, prefer the simple beauty provided by Mother Nature herself.

Quartz is the largest of the crystal families, and we can be grateful for that since it is such a powerful healer. Moreover, it is an energy regulator for the human body, affecting the vibrations of the *aura,* or energy field that surrounds all living beings.

# Defining Crystal Categories

First, let's explain the different categories: precious and semiprecious gems, crystals, and stones. We'll start with the widest category, stones, which actually encompasses all the other categories. Stones can hold much magic and bring the best to you. I'm always looking in my path for a pretty stone or one of an unusual shape or coloration. In fact, I have a mobile altar in my car that is frequently augmented by a charming chunk of rock. I always notice that my friends and passengers are unable to resist picking them up and rubbing the smooth surfaces admiringly. Maybe one day, I'll find a diamond in the rough in my path!

Stones have been of interest for many centuries. Primitive peoples probably picked up stones out of curiosity. Through trial and error, they discovered which rocks withstood the test of time and were more durable for use in tools. Doubtless, they also noticed that some stones could be polished to a lovely sheen.

Stones are primarily minerals that can be defined as natural, generally inorganic substances with a chemical composition and an internal atomic structure. So, a diamond, the most precious of all in the eyes of many rock hounds, is a stone and also a crystal with a very simple structure of one element —carbon. Quartz, a very commonly available and rarely expensive stone, is usually referred to as rock crystal and is composed of two elements—silicon and oxygen. Crystals are defined as such because of their internal diffracting patterns—that is, by the way they hold and reflect light. Rocks can be defined as natural, solid compounds of mineral grains or glass, or a combination of both.

What is the difference between precious and semiprecious gems? The simple distinction between these two categories is that only the most rare and costly gems are classified as precious. Emeralds, rubies, sapphires, and diamonds fall into this foremost category. Those remaining gems, such as opal, amethyst, and bloodstone, are semiprecious. Gems are a special class of very valuable minerals rated according to their hardness, color, and luster. Gems are held so dear because of their quality; they are usually clearer, rarer, and exquisitely beautiful.

All of these "rules" date back thousands of years in some cases. There is a great tradition surrounding the lore and love of gems, stones, and crystals. They are simply glorious. Think about it—not only are they lovely to look at and to adorn yourself with, but they also have properties that bring love, health, happiness, abundance, and peace of mind.

## THE MYSTIQUE OF MINERALS

Each gem, mineral, crystal, and stone discussed in this volume has its own unique properties. Look at it this way: We have a vast healing and life-enhancing trove of beautiful and sacred stones from which to choose, and each stone has its own inherent, divine qualities. Each one is unique for the energy it emits and how it interacts with our subtle energy field, or aura. In the same way that no two fingerprints or snowflakes are alike, each crystal is completely individual, never to be repeated again in nature. Man-made crystals are exactly alike, thus reducing their appeal and healing qualities, at least in my mind.

Crystals found in nature are imbued with special qualities from the minerals and rocks surrounding them. Geologists are fond of explaining the varying colors of crystals as chemical impurities, and while that may well be so, I prefer to liken the development of crystalline color to the making of a fine wine, wherein the soil and even neighboring trees, plants, sun, and rain affect the grapes and the resulting nectar. So, gems have notes, like a perfume or a wine or even music. Truly gifted gemologists can distinguish these delicate differences, especially the vibratory sounds.

# MAKING MAGIC WITH GEMS

Gems are powerful tools that can pave the way for a better life for you! There is a long history of the use of gems, stones, and crystals as amulets, symbols, charms, and jewelry in magic. These myriad stones can really enrich your life in so many ways. In the next chapter, you will learn how to make your own magical gem and crystal jewelry and how to charge the stones you already own with supernatural power.

Do you want to get a new job? Jade jewelry magic will do the trick! Need to get over a heartbreak? A chrysocolla heart-healing spell will soothe your soul. Are you an author suffering the dreaded writer's block? A creativity crystal incantation is exactly what you need.

Gems and statues positioned in strategic places around your home can help accelerate the positive vibrations you are activating by practicing gem magic. Using what I call crystal feng shui, you can place a crystal or a geode or an appealingly shaped rock in the appropriate position of your home to facilitate change. For example, amethyst will promote healing and release any negative energy that is clinging. Clusters of citrine will activate vibrations of abundance and creativity.

So, if you want to bring more money into your home or office, place a big chunk of citrine on the left side of your desk, and the money will begin to flow! If you have a dark hallway that feels spooky or an area in your home or office in which the energy feels very static or low, place an obsidian ball there, perhaps in a pedestal, to absorb this negative energy. If you want to have your bedroom be a place of bliss and unconditional love, rose quartz will create this all-important atmosphere.

Crystal magic also involves color magic and spell craft, topics that are covered in depth herein. With gem magic, you will learn to improve your life in ways large and small. You will discover the stones that are special to you and how to fully utilize these birthstones and karmic crystals. You will undertake the magical arts of crystal conjuring and spell casting with stones. You will be inducted into the practice of healing with crystals and how to achieve wellness every day. Finally, you will have at your fingertips the history, description, and instructions on how to use each and every gem and crystal.

Using gems and crystals in rituals, spells, and affirmations has been a part of the human experience for millennia. By incorporating this practice into your life, you will create a flow of positive energy that will enable you to enhance your work, your family, your love, and every other part of your existence.

Yes, through the magic of gems, anything is possible. Again, welcome to this glittering and magical realm and begin a special journey under a sky where every star is a jewel you can wish upon!

## Tips 'n' Tricks

### CRYSTALLINE CATALYST

If you are reading this book, it is a good sign that you are wanting positive change in your life. Crystals and gems are powerful vehicles for creating advantageous new directions for you to try. Certain crystals are *revolutionary rocks*—they can bring fresh change in your life NOW. Moonstone stimulates all the senses. Onyx helps with self-control. Peridot balances the physical energies. Sapphire is a motivator. Pink quartz helps overcome bad habits. Bloodstone rids emotional blockage. Alexandrite encourages love for life.

*Chapter Two*

# GEM AND JEWELRY MAGIC

Gem magic is where we are at play in the fields of the gods and goddesses who have given us these unimaginably beautiful gifts. We can ornament ourselves with gems and can also direct the inherent energy contained in these stones through the basics of gem magic. In this section, you will discover precious minerals and metals and how you can begin to develop your skills as a gem magician. Your jewelry box can become a treasure chest filled with enchantments once you have begun. Your amethyst earrings can become intuition boosters that will help you advance at work. Your citrine necklace can awaken an inner knowing and help you access your Goddess-given intelligence more fully. Your grandmother's antique ruby ring can become a beacon for attracting love in your life. Shall we begin?

## PRECIOUS AND SEMIPRECIOUS STONES

Gemstones are cherished for their incredible durability and eternal beauty. The variety of gems is quite wide, but the U.S. Trade Commission lists only emeralds, natural rubies, diamonds, and sapphires as precious gemstones. All others are considered semiprecious, which seems a bit limited to me but is nonetheless the rule of thumb, according to governmental authorities. Rubies, if unflawed and of a perfect, deep red, are the most valuable of all gems, being the least available. Emeralds are next, and diamonds, perhaps surprisingly, are the last in line of this precious trio. Interestingly, the ancient Egyptians actually valued semiprecious stones more. The Egyptians made a vast study of gems of all kinds, and the earliest writing of any kind about these sacred stones was found on papyrus dating back to 1500 B.C.

Gems have fascinated and played important roles in the lives of historical figures from alchemists to biblical scholars. The famous philosopher's stone is, of course, purported to be a gem of enormous power and significance. Gem lore tells us that a stone can also have the power to throw a life into disarray. Marie Antoinette lost her head as a result of the public outcry over a purloined diamond necklace, and everyone who owned the Hope diamond either died before their time or was bankrupted until it was donated to the Smithsonian Institution.

Bearing these examples in mind, just know that stones carry energy, and if they are stolen or ill-gotten, the energy clinging to the stones can greatly impact the owners and wearers. Being honorable is essential when you are wielding stone power. Having said that, the pleasures of owning and working with gemstones can be enormous. Gems can adorn your hand and help make you wiser. A gem-power pendant can open your heart to love and give you greater happiness than you have ever known. Gem power can heal your body and clear your mind.

## Tips 'n' Tricks

### FAIRY FLINT

Flint is favored by the fairy folk. If you want to be on the good side of the wee ones, keep flint around, and they will go about their own business and not meddle in yours. No more lost car keys or misplaced wallets after that!

# Magical Jewelry

A marvelous way to take fuller advantage of the power of your gems and crystals is to wear them in jewelry. Even better, you can make the jewelry you own magical by *charging* it—imbuing it with intention and purpose and power. Also, you can craft your own magical jewelry, which is perhaps the most powerful option of all because you hold your desires in mind as you put your enchantments together step by step and gem by gem.

As you wear a gem, you're not only decorating yourself but also experiencing its interaction with your energy systems. A large portion of this book is devoted to explaining the energies of each of the major crystals and gems along with some of the rarer rocks, so you must read through the descriptionary part to determine which stones are best for you. Not all will be, by any means, and some will conflict with your personal energy, as I also point out herein. Give a lot of thought about what constructive changes you wish to see in your life or what good qualities you want to develop further in yourself.

For example, right now, I want to get more organized, so I will get some lazulite. Of course, getting organized requires some letting go and getting rid of stuff. This is a real problem for me. As any of my friends can tell you, I have paper issues, and my North Beach cottage is lined with magazines, journals, and books, books, books! But, I *really* feel the need to declutter my life and stream-line it—get a bit more Zen. So, I'll have to get organized with lazulite power and then let go with lepidolite! Also, I have never really had any jade, but recently, I feel like I need the grounding and stabilizing effects of this stone. Additionally, I need to get more prosperity-minded. I need to be better about saving money and thinking in terms of my future security so I'm not reading tarot out on the sidewalk when I'm 90! So, I have been walking through San Francisco's

Chinatown and feeling very attracted to different jades. I'm sure you feel such urges and attractions, too. Often, this might be your subconscious giving you a gentle nudge about some growing you need to do. Listen to those inner voices, and you will reap the benefits again and again.

## CHARGING YOUR JEWELRY WITH MAGIC

Charging a gem or crystal imbues it with your intent. Upon charging your jewelry, you can use it in spell work or anytime you want to surround yourself with the magic you put into the gemstones. While picturing your truest wish and hope, and what you ultimately want to achieve through this process, anoint a candle with an essential oil that most expresses your energy. Perhaps it is rose or, as in my case, amber. Begin by lighting the candle and gazing into the flame. Then, place the piece of jewelry in front of the candle and say aloud, "Into this jewelry, I imbue my essence and the power of this blessed earth. This gem of great hue is charged until my magic is through. So mote it be!"

You can further empower the jewel by scratching your desire into the wax of the candle. Then, each time you burn the candle, place the gem before it and think upon your quest.

To enchant all of your jewelry, you need to create an altar for this express purpose. You can prepare the way for letting gem magic into your life, and focusing your desires and dreams, with a gem-magic altar. If you already have an altar in place, incorporate some of the following elements. The more you use your altar, the more powerful your spells will be.

Your gem-magic altar can be a low table, the top of a chest, or even a shelf. First, you must purify the space with the smoke of a sage bundle. This is called smudging and is essential in clearing energy to make way for magic. You can use wild sage or purchase it at any herb store or metaphysical five-and-dime.

Once you have smudged the space, cover your altar with your favorite fabric; I recommend the color white. Place a candle in each corner. I prefer candles of many colors to represent the rainbow array of gems. Place gems and crystals of your choice around the candles. Rose quartz is a heart stone, and fluorite is a calming crystal, so these are good choices for grounding yourself, particularly if your altar is in your bedroom, as many are! Add to the altar fresh flowers, an incense you simply love to smell, and any objects that have special meaning to you. Some folks place lovely shells or feathers they have found in their paths or on the beach, and others use imagery that is special—a goddess statue or a star shape. The most important point is that your altar be pleasing to your eye and your sensibilities. You should feel that it represents the deepest aspects of you as a person.

Ideally, you will bless your altar on a new moon. Light the candles and incense, and say aloud:

> *"Here burns happiness about me,*
>
> *Peace and harmony are in abundance,*
>
> *Here my happiness abounds.*
>
> *Gems and jewels—these bones of the earth*
>
> *Bring love, prosperity, health, and mirth.*
>
> *Be it ever thus that joy is the light*
>
> *That here burns bright.*
>
> *Blessed be!"*

You have now consecrated your altar. It will ease your spirit anytime and become your power source. Your altar connects you to the earth of which you and all gems and crystals are a part. Your altar will connect you to the gem magic that has now entered your life. Whenever you want to add a dash of magic or a supernatural sparkle to a stone or piece of jewelry, you can place it on your altar for seven days. On the seventh day, wear the jewelry and bewitch everyone you encounter! Remember that your level of clarity and concentration will be reflected in the jewel's power.

Now, enjoy your sacred stones.

# THE LANGUAGE OF JEWELRY

A little thoughtfulness about how and where to wear your crystal and gem jewelry can go a long way toward enhancing your health and happiness. The left side of your body is the most sensitive, or *feeling*, side; the right side is your *action* side. Information and energy flow into your left side much more quickly, so you can protect yourself by wearing crystals on that side that act as energy guards. Jewelry worn on the right side of your body helps with work, productivity, and success.

## *Necklaces, Pendants, and Chokers*

Perhaps you want to be a better communicator or to sing or simply to express yourself more freely. A blocked throat chakra can result in your feelings and ideas being blocked. So, in this case, you will want to focus on opening up the throat chakra. A necklace or choker can serve this purpose. A strand of pearls not only looks timelessly elegant but also boosts your self-esteem and sociability. The best metals for this use are silver, copper, and gold. You will want to avoid aluminum entirely because it is considered to be a health risk.

## Earrings

You can wear one gold earring and one silver earring to rid yourself of the discomfort of a headache. Earrings were once worn to guard ears from potential disease and from hearing bad news. They were also believed to strengthen weak eyes, especially if set with emeralds. Earrings help to balance both hemispheres of the brain and can also stabilize the throat chakra. The earlobes are sensory centers on the body and usually benefit from the stimulation of a gem or crystal. Jade and tiger's-eye are great for reviving and refreshing. You will generally feel quite good with these two earring choices. Sapphires will bring you greater wisdom. However, lapis lazuli and opal can be overstimulating as earrings, so watch carefully and see how your body reacts to them. Some people feel light-headed with these two stones placed so high on the body. Malachite can be too spiritually stimulating as earrings; don't wear them unless you want to be in a soulful or dreamy reverie. Go for garnet, as garnet earrings will enhance your popularity. And here is a tip that might soon cause a stampede to the jewelry shop: Rose quartz is wonderful for the skin and can even slow aging!

## Chains

Chains represent links between people, the ties that bind you to another. Other mystical associations for chains are happiness and justice; prayer; reason and the soul; communication and command. Plato referred to a *chain of being,* a golden chain linking the earth to the heavens above, a bond between humans and immortals. Socrates tied our human happiness to the concept of justice with a chain of steel and diamonds. Pseudo-Dionysius the Areopagite compared the practice of prayer to an infinitely luminous chain going from Earth to heaven. An astral cord, akin to a golden chain, binds the spirit to the psyche and binds reason to the soul.

## Tips 'n' Tricks

### SPEAKING STONES

If you are a singer or speaker or simply wish to improve how you express yourself, wear these stones in chokers or necklaces to realize a noticeable change for the better: amber, amethyst, aquamarine, azurite, blue obsidian, blue topaz, blue tourmaline, kunzite, lepidolite, and turquoise.

## Rings

Rings represent eternity, unity, reincarnation, safety, union, power, and energy. They symbolize the eternity of the circle shape—the universe. Wearing rings was believed to help ward off any kind of malevolence through their continuity —nothing could get in. A ring binds you with the energy of the stone. In dream psychology, a ring represents the desire for reconciliation of the different parts of your being and personality; it shows you want to be an integrated whole, which is the first step in making it happen. If you want to deepen a friendship, exchange amber rings with your friend to bind you together forever. Why do you think Native Americans wear turquoise rings? They know it is a guardian stone; its power is doubled when it is in a ring.

When wearing a ring, be sure the bottom side of the stone is open to allow greater connection between the stone and your skin. On your left hand, wear ring gems that awaken and release emotions, and on your right hand, wear stones that will enhance your career and your personal goals in life. I know that thumb rings have become a big trend, but you should know that wearing them could block the energy of the thumbs or, even worse, bring out egotism and selfishness.

Your index fingers are indicators of achievement, and wearing the proper gem on that finger can really aid you in striving for your dreams. For wisdom, wear lapis lazuli. For greater love of yourself and others, try pearl, moonstone, or garnet. For success, wear carnelian. For a quiet mind and greater calm, wear sodalite, chrysocolla, or turquoise.

Your middle fingers are about ideas and insight as well as intuition; the left hand represents the receiving of ideas, and the right hand represents action and achievement in your life. Wear stones on the middle finger only when you want to get a lot of psychic input from the world around you. For greater sensitivity and creativity, wear amethyst. To awaken your inner and outer beauty, wear ruby. To access your higher good and know your life purpose, wear sapphire or quartz crystal.

The ring finger is about creativity, and, of course, the ring finger on the left hand is your love center and a direct connection to your heart. For deep and loyal ties of love, wear diamond. To express your love, wear moonstone. To inspire creativity, wear emerald. To meet creativity goals, wear tiger's-eye or cat's-eye. For practicality in your work and art, wear turquoise. For service to your community and the world, wear opal. For serenity both within and without, wear ruby.

Pinkie fingers represent change. The right gem on your little finger can help you find and pursue new opportunities and change the direction of your whole life. This is a lot of power in one little ring! For better organizational habits, wear pearl. For unwinding and simplifying, wear turquoise. To bring new energy and new prospects, wear aventurine.

## A MUSE-ICAL WAND

If your passion is making art or music, throwing pots, or growing an artful garden, you are an imaginative person, and you need to stay in touch with your muse. Call her to you anytime you are feeling blocked or uninspired. You can make a very special tool that will draw your muse to you with sweet-smelling smoke.

You'll want to keep a pot of the hardy and sun-loving herb sage on your windowsill so it is handy at all times. Here is a simple way to use this herb to create a wand for instant inspiration: Combine a long stalk of fennel with a twisted bundle of sage and long sticks of your favorite incense, such as cinnamon or nag champa (my personal favorite). Braid the materials tightly together into a wand using purple (for power) and gold (for money) string or thread. Before any artistic endeavor or meditation, light one end of the wand with a candle and wave it around to clear your environment, allowing the smoke to clear your mind in the process.

### Brooches

Brooches symbolize virginity, faithfulness, and protection. A diamond-studded brooch is a double symbol of love and safeguarding.

Brooches were the costume jewelry of the medieval Irish, who decorated themselves with gems and valuable stones to show they were part of the aspiring warrior caste.

### Headdresses

It is no accident that kings, queens, and emperors wear crowns. The ancients wanted their leaders to be wise, and bejeweled crowns brought the energy of gems to bear on their brows. While you might not want to wear a tiara to the office, you can wear hair clips and barrettes with crystals and stones attached for some of the same reasons. Why not be smarter and smartly accessorized?

I loved it when *bindis* (the "dots" traditionally worn by Indian women on their foreheads) came back into vogue, because jewels on the *third eye* (an invisible organ of spiritual perception) stimulate intuition and compassion. Wear bindis in moderation, however, to avoid exhausting your center of intuition.

### Bracelets

I love bracelets and am wearing an aventurine cuff right now. The wrists are perfect pulse points. Organic gems, such as coral and abalone, are very helpful for energy flow and release. Turquoise is great for stabilizing and calming you physically.

Ancient cultures loved to wear armbands and cuffs, and those have gone out of style except among the most dramatic of fashionistas. Perhaps we should try to bring this style back because gem and crystal armbands are very good for body and soul.

## Tips 'n' Tricks

### A POCKETFUL OF KRYPTONITE

While making a gemstone belt or waist chain could be a major investment of time and money, placing a rock in your pocket is a quick and easy way to bring change into your life! To get a new job, carry tourmaline, moss agate, tiger's-eye, or carnelian. If you're looking for love, pocket a moonstone. For money, carry green jade.

## Tips 'n' Tricks

### PEARLS FOR PATIENCE

In this fast-paced world, we are so accustomed to instant gratification—high-speed Internet connection, same-day delivery. We are multitasking ourselves to death. Slow down and enjoy your life. It is worth it, I assure you. Here is a quick way to simply relax and enjoy the little things of life: Wear a pearl. Pearl earrings and necklaces are the best, as they calm and clear the mind.

### Belts

Waist jewelry has recently made a big comeback. People are going beyond belts and wearing belly chains and lariats. Gemstone belts and buckles can really enhance your joie de vivre and give you greater physical strength and health. Turquoise stones are grounding, and agates raise the energy level. For healing power, try bloodstone. For keeping life on an even keel, the organic-gem family—shells, corals, and abalone—is optimal. For impetus and motivation, wear carnelian. To boost your health and well-being, wear red coral for the lungs, bloodstone for the heart, and moonstone during pregnancy.

### Ankle Bracelets and Toe Rings

Bejeweled feet and ankles are very sexy. Jewelry in this area of the body is also grounding and stabilizing. If you are dealing with anxiety or substance-abuse issues, wear amethyst around your ankle. If you're feeling drained of energy, jasper or rock crystal will come in handy. Rhodonite will do the trick if you are feeling disconnected or restless.

**THE SALT OF THE EARTH**

You can cleanse all of your jewelry by placing it into a bowl of sea salt for seven days to make sure nobody else's energy is permeating the pieces. This is especially helpful if you own antique or estate jewelry.

# Making Marvelous Jewelry

## Twinkle-Star Toe Ring

Every step you take will be supernatural when you wear your Twinkle-Star Toe Ring! To make this ring, you'll need forty-four tiny amethyst beads, 18 inches of elastic thread, two sewing needles or two wire thread needles, and glue. Once you get the knack of the project, you can try it again and vary the number and type of crystal beads.

Begin by blessing the beads on your altar. Next, thread the needles onto each end of the elastic thread and then string four beads to the center of the elastic. Thread the left needle through the last bead on the right-hand side. Pull it tight, forming a diamond shape. Next, string one bead on the left thread end and two beads on the right. Thread the left needle through the last bead on the right. Pull it tight. Repeat until all the beads are used. In order to close the ring, thread the left needle through the end bead of the first diamond, instead of the last bead on the right. Pull tight, tie the ring off with a double knot, and place a drop of glue on the knot.

Notice how everyone is looking at you as you sparkle by? You are irresistible!

## Rings of Power

You can follow the exact steps above to make yourself finger rings that can bring more grace and less grief into your life. Think about the different areas of your life and then create an entire collection of rings to sprinkle a little magic into those areas.

Study the descriptionary in Part Two of this book, and you can explore and discover dozens of marvelous stones from which to choose. Do you want to be more creative? Try tiger's-eye. Need to find a job? Plume agate is your stone. Looking to add some pizzazz to your love life? Alexandrite will bring lots of zest. Feeling blue? Citrine or jet can banish dark days. Stressed out? Rhyolite races to the rescue!

## Gem-Magic Get-Together

Forget the Tupperware party and have a gem-magic party with your girlfriends instead. Make popcorn, eat pizza, drink champagne, and, most importantly, make magic together. What could be more fun? All you have to do is pick a night and assign everyone two ingredients to bring—one snack and one batch of crystal beads. You provide the thread, tools, glue, and good vibes.

Think about beginning the night by making brooches. A brooch worn over the heart is a symbol of loyalty and love among friends. You'll need to get some flat-circle brooch pins at a craft store. Give each person at the party a brooch and ask her to choose a partner. Using glue, each gal will encrust the front of her brooch with as many crystals as possible in a color and an array that best represent the personality of her partner. Then, the partners exchange brooches. Your gaggle of girlfriends will be forever bonded by their love brooches, not to mention the glue!

Here are a few other festive and fun projects you can whip up together: birthstone bracelets, bewitching barrettes, pendulum pendants, true-love tiaras, blessing bracelets, bodacious bobby pins, and nights-of-enchantment necklaces. The possibilities are endless; let your imagination (and your friends) run wild!

## Seven Sacred Stones Bracelet

Take any silver chain-link bracelet and add "charm" to it! Bracelets act as protection jewelry, and, well, they look simply divine on our delicate wrists, do they not? Of late, the trend has been to layer bracelets, but with gem magic, there's a danger that jeweled pieces worn together could cancel each other out because they have conflicting energies. So, I am going to recommend that you wear this bracelet alone, without other magical wrist wear.

To make this piece, you'll need seven stones on small pendant settings, a silver chain-link bracelet, seven jump rings, and pliers. Plain silver chain-link

## Tips 'n' Tricks

### WEAR THIS AT WORK

Geode jewelry can bring you success at work. At my favorite metaphysical five-and-dimes, I have been seeing baby geodes that can easily be glued to a fabric choker band or are already in premade pendants. If you are feeling like you are in a slump at work or want to impress the boss, begin wearing a pretty and professional geode necklace and things will be looking up soon! If this style is not for you, just buy a geode, set it on your desk, and look at it while picturing yourself climbing the ladder of success.

bracelets are easy to obtain at any jewelry department or store, from Target to Tiffany. Jump rings, which have an opening through which you can slide a pendant and then close up with small chain-nose pliers, are readily available at any craft or jewelry store.

Before you choose your seven stones, decide what energy enhancement you desire. If you want lots of energy and zest, choose red jasper or pink clamshell. If you want to be uplifted, try jade. To become wiser, pick sapphire. To stay safe while traveling, pick dendritic agate. To remain calm and overcome stress, choose blue lace agate. For more mental clarity, choose malachite. For a self-esteem boost, try rhodonite.

Once you have perused all the gem and crystal descriptions in this book, you can and should experiment with all manner of combinations. But I highly recommend the Seven Sacred Stones Bracelet with the following very beneficial stones and energies:

+ **citrine** for a better ability to communicate,
+ **lace agate** for happiness with your job,
+ **lapis lazuli** for mental brilliance,
+ **moonstone** for self-love and self-expression,
+ **red coral** for good health and physical strength,
+ **rose quartz or opal** to make you appealing to others, and
+ **turquoise** for calmness and protection from the earth.

Friends of mine have reported wonderful results with this banishing and boosting bracelet. Where else can you find jewelry that will make you feel good about yourself, protect you from harm, and help you to look even prettier? You have to make it! You can find these pendant-set stones in any jewelry or New Age store. The metaphysical stores have the best selection, however.

To begin, place the stones on your altar or in front of a candle for six days and six nights. Write on a piece of paper or parchment what you desire from each stone. While you light the candle each night, think about and meditate upon all the wonderful things you want in your life. On the seventh day, loop each pendant stone onto your bracelet with even spacing. Burn the parchment with the candle flame and then put your bracelet on and jingle it seven times. From now on, every time you hear the seven sacred stones jingle on your wrist, think about the qualities the stones are bringing you and you'll refresh the gem magic.

## Choker of Charm

This "floating" crystal choker seems magical because the gems appear to hover around your lovely neck all by themselves. And maybe sometimes they do! The secret, aside from the magical gems, is the invisible thread, easily obtained at any craft store. The purpose of the Choker of Charm is to make you simply irresistible to whomever you wish to attract. Wake your boyfriend up with this enchanted choker, or hit the town with your friend and notice how a crowd develops around YOU!

You'll need these ingredients: twenty-one crystal beads, 22 inches of invisible thread, a lobster-claw clasp, and glue.

First, tie one end of the invisible thread to the loop in the lobster-claw clasp, also readily available at any craft store and most jewelry stores. Knot the thread twice, add a drop of glue, and allow the thread to dry. Clip off the extra thread after the glue has dried. Then, string three beads onto the thread about three-quarters of an inch from the clasp and tie a knot in the thread beside the beads. Repeat until you've used all the beads. There will be seven groups of three, and each group of crystals should be evenly separated. At the last bead, tie the end of the thread to the clasp ring.

Here are a few irresistible crystals to consider using in your Choker of Charm:

+ **Amazonite** makes you hopeful.
+ **Amber** boosts your spirits—you will feel good!
+ **Aventurine** creates good opportunities.
+ **Banded agate** attracts a lover of strength and courage.
+ **Brown jasper** makes you confident and emotionally secure.
+ **Opal** enhances beauty and makes you more psychic.
+ **Pearl** augments femininity.

# Magic Metals

Just as the first humans sensed that stones contained energy and special properties, so too they found that metals boasted energies that had tremendous influence and power. Metals used to be very commonplace in magic, but their popularity has lessened within the last 500 years, after alchemists began to turn into scientists.

Magical metallurgy has rebounded a bit and plays a definite role in gem magic. The simplest way to employ magic metals is to place a copper penny in your pocket or carry a pouch containing a horseshoe nail for luck. Mystical metals—from bewitching bronze to supernatural silver—can add a whole dimension to gem magic in your life.

### Gold

Gold is beloved for its sheen and purity. Whether white or yellow, it is a fantastic energy conductor. Gold enhances any gem or stone and encourages the action of said stone with a dose of quickening energy. It is a symbol of wealth and personal power and accentuates any gem or crystal. Gold also accentuates *you*.

The softest and the strongest metal, gold never tarnishes and seems to stay beautiful and perfect through anything; it's impermeable to weather and the effects of aging. This is an adaptable, mutable metal and maintains its unity in alloys.

Gold fascinates—no doubt about it. It is used in jewelry, in industry, and also in medicine. Because gold is a viable energy conductor, it has wonderful healing properties, and because it is impervious to harm, gold is a tremendous element of renewal and regeneration. It has been said to help with arthritis, blood and circulation problems, chemical and hormone imbalances, stress-related illnesses, pulmonary problems, and mental and emotional issues.

Gold can give you courage and self-esteem. It can accentuate the positive in yourself and your regard of others. Wearing gold-nugget jewelry might even bring in a continuous flow of wealth!

In Mexico, gold is linked to religion and faith. Gold crucifixes and crosses are worn for protection and as a link to God, Christ, and Mary. In India, parents give their young children tiny gold amulets to guard against harm and illness.

Let this metal of kings and queens cast a golden glow over your life!

*Tips 'n' Tricks*

## JEWELS OF WISDOM

- Agate worn as an amulet around your neck will ensure that you will speak only your truth. It can also attract favors from powerful people!
- A black agate on a short chain or in a ring will ensure success in business and athletics.
- If you wear moss agate while gardening, you will have a healthy harvest.

- If you wear amazonite while gambling, you will have great luck.
- Amber will attract love into your life and increase sensual pleasure if you wear it during lovemaking.
- If a man wears an amethyst, the stone will draw a good woman to him.
- Apache tear in a pendant will protect a woman in her pregnancy.
- Frog-shaped jewelry is the ultimate traveler's amulet; pilots, stewards, sailors, and anyone who frequently travels across water should wear aquamarine in frog-shaped jewelry for enhanced safety and protection from drowning.
- Wear bloodstone in court for victory in legal matters.
- Carnelian jewelry will keep you from being struck by lightning.
- Cat's-eye worn as a ring will retain your youthful beauty and lift any depression.
- Ladies, coral earrings will attract men into your life. Pacific Islanders believe this "nature's jewel" contains the very essence of life.
- A diamond with a six-sided cut will offer you great protection; set in platinum, it will ensure victory in any conflict.
- Jade carved into the shape of a butterfly will attract love into your life.
- Lapis lazuli beads strung on gold wire will offer health, growth, and protection.
- A diamond set in onyx will overcome sexual temptation and incite the loyalty of a partner.
- Opal earrings will awaken your psychic powers.
- A red pearl ring or pendant will heighten intelligence.
- A dark peridot ring will bring you more money and raise your sprits, allaying any melancholy.
- A geode as jewelry will attract love and help a woman avoid miscarriage.

## Silver

Aligned with the planet and the god Mercury, silver is about communication. Silver has been associated with the moon for thousands of years. As such, it is a stabilizer of any crystal or gem. Rather than adding to the energy of a stone, it secures the energy and supports the gem.

## *Tips 'n' Tricks*

### SOWING THE SEEDS OF CHANGE

Nature is the ultimate creator. Get an array of seed packets, and plant newness in your life. If your thumb is not the greenest, I suggest nasturtiums, which will grow in any soil and seem to thrive on neglect.

On a new-moon day, draw a square in your yard or planter with a natural wand—a willow branch or an oak stick, for example—and mark each corner with a candle and a stone:

- ◆ orange candle and stone for higher intelligence (onyx or jasper),
- ◆ green candle and stone for creativity and growth (jade, peridot, or malachite),
- ◆ blue candle and stone for serenity and goodness (lapis lazuli, turquoise, or celestite),
- ◆ white candle and stone for purification (Herkimer diamond, quartz, or limestone).

Repeat this chant as you light each candle:

> *"Great Gaia, I turn to you to help me renew,*
> *Under this new moon and in this old earth. Blessed be."*

Poke the seeds under the soil with your fingers and tamp them down with your wand. Gently water your new-moon garden, and affirmative change will begin that very day.

Silver is a healing metal that should *not* be worn all the time; let your body tell you when it feels right. Silver offers a mirror of your inner spirit, and this should be given very special attention. Silver is a detoxifying agent and communicates with the body to alert you to raised levels of hormones and other chemical imbalances. The metal is good to wear as a necklace, as it is very beneficial to the throat and lungs. Your synapses even fire more efficiently because silver acts as an energy conductor. Consequently, silver is good for people encountering memory reduction, psychological issues, and diseases affecting the brain.

In olden days, women wore silver around their waists to improve fertility. Men can do the same—by wearing a silver belt buckle, perhaps—to treat impotence or any other sexual dysfunction.

Moonstones are wonderful in combination with the sacred moon metal. Amethyst is also great in a silver setting. Jaspers, agates (especially fire agate), and opals are very suitable in silver. Although diamonds are more often set in gold, they are also terrific in silver settings. The same holds true for sapphires. Lapis, jades, emeralds, and pearls set in silver are said to attract love.

Here is a list of stones you should *not* set in silver: zircon, tourmaline, and amber. I see amber set in silver all the time, and it is unfortunate because amber is a *hot* stone and works better with any other metal.

In foreign countries, silver is used in a variety of customary ways. Parents in China, for example, give their children silver-locket necklaces to show love and offer protection and luck. In France, couples wear silver chains upon getting engaged.

## Copper

This is the metal most consciously worn as a healer, as evidenced by the many copper bracelets you see on wrists. If worn on the left side of the body, copper is thought to have the power to actually prevent sickness. The latest fad I've noticed has golfers embracing copper to help strengthen their wrists to improve their swings. Healers place their faith in copper's power to heal the body and mind based on its power as a conductor. Copper supports and reinforces the mineral content of gems and crystals so they interact better with your body. One school of thought propounds the belief that a crystal wand wound with copper is super-powered. You will notice that some of the healing rocks discussed in this book have copper as a trace element, which greatly amps up their power. Some of these

## Tips 'n' Tricks

### WRITTEN IN STONE

Gems and crystals can give us messages and warnings or powers of persuasion and perception. Here are a few examples:

- ◆ A fossil or a gem containing a fossil, such as amber, will lengthen your life span.
- ◆ Jasper carved into the shape of an arrow will be a magnet for good luck.
- ◆ If your malachite jewelry chips or breaks, beware! It is warning you of danger.
- ◆ Malachite gives great success to salespeople. Keep a malachite crystal in the cash register and wear it during trade shows, presentations, and meetings.
- ◆ Moonstone is the dieter's power stone and helps maintain youthful appearances and attitudes.
- ◆ Serpentine worn around a new mother's neck helps her flow of milk.

copper-ore gemstones are azurite, chrysocolla, malachite, and turquoise. Copper reacts best with stones containing a lot of metal and reacts very little with stones that lack metal ore in their makeup. Tiger's-eye, aventurine, rhodonite, and mica are metal-rich stones whose energies combine beautifully with copper. Do *not* place most crystalline stones in copper; the same holds true with pearls and coral. Amethyst is one of the only crystalline stones that will work well with copper. Copper also cooperates with gold and silver, and a multimetal bracelet with the right stone is a powerful piece for healing!

Copper is found around the world and has been utilized since ancient times for tools, for decoration, and for jewelry. It has played a significant role in the cultures of the Greeks and Romans, Native Americans, Egyptians, and peoples in India, China, and Japan. Copper, which is ruled by Venus, was believed to be able to protect against evil and is said to attract love, especially if set with emeralds. The Egyptians relied upon copper for the ritual of burying the dead. Copper is deeply ingrained in our human history for its use as sacred knives, candleholders in early churches, Asian prayer diagrams, purification vessels, and countless other holy instruments.

This metal stimulates the flow of energy throughout the body and also the mind. Anyone who suffers from lethargy should wear copper to get out of his or her rut. That reminds me—where are my copper bracelet and wand? Copper is believed to be a helpmate to the body's blood, soft tissue, immune system, metabolism, and mucous membranes. It has also been credited with being a purifier, lending feelings of freedom and possibility, and having positive effects on self-esteem, communication skills, and confidence levels. Even better, it is known as a lucky metal, and you'll be twice as lucky if you combine it with cat's-eye, coral, opal, or Apache tear. Quite frankly, who could ask for anything more?

## Brass

Brass is the result of combining copper and zinc. You may be surprised to learn that brass has been used successfully to treat hair loss! Healers favor it as a detoxifier and cleanser for people who have too much metal in their bloodstreams. Brass is also a strengthening alloy for the body and supports gems and crystals in their energies and abilities to interact in a positive way with your body. The iron content in the brass is what makes it a real stabilizer. The healing and protective powers of brass are enhanced if it is worn as a brooch in the shape of a dog, falcon, or snake.

Brass is a wealth attractor and has often been used as a shiny substitute for the much more costly gold. The ancients *loved* placing their gems in brass for the way it made the beautiful colors really stand out.

## Bronze

Bronze is also an alloy of zinc and copper and has the same healing power as brass but with one exception—bronze is said to give greater strength of character. My favorite aspect of bronze is that it helps folks conceive of and achieve their goals.

## Platinum

Platinum is an extremely precious metal and makes for a very special setting for gems and jewels. Careful consideration must be given to what crystals are placed into a platinum setting, as they need to have energies that can stand up to the high energy of this metal. Diamonds have a strong enough brilliance, and their power is enhanced when set in platinum. Ruby, tourmaline, sapphire, and emerald are other good choices for platinum settings.

# Living the Magic

Now you have been initiated into the art of gem magic. You can make yourself a true-love tiara, a seductive toe ring, or a bewitching bracelet, to name but a few of the crystalline conjuring projects you have in your new bag of tricks. Gem magic is a merry way to make magic, but it is, in essence, all about improving the quality of your life. These gorgeous gems and sacred stones are all around us, with enhancing energies that you can apply consciously to bring a sense of well-being to your job, your family, your friends, your love life, and your deepest spirit and psyche. Use gem magic to create wonder, fun, fantasy, and fulfillment in all areas of your life.

## *Tips 'n' Tricks*

### MIXING CRYSTALS

Here are some tips about stones *not* to mix together in jewelry, as their energies cancel each other out:

◆ Carnelian counteracts amethyst, as it connects more strongly with the body.

◆ Lapis lazuli stimulates the mind, and blue lace agate relaxes it.

◆ Lapis lazuli and turquoise are also opposites, although I can't help but notice that this didn't stop the Egyptians from using them together!

◆ Turquoise dampens the energy of malachite.

◆ Diamonds and turquoise have such different energies that they conflict.

*Chapter Three*

# BIRTHSTONES
# AND
# ASTROGEMOLOGY

**B**irthstones are the very special stones that have traditionally been correlated with every month of the year. Hallmark didn't invent the concept of birthstones, however; it came from the Bible! In Exodus chapters 28 and 39, there is much discussion about a burnished and stone-set breastplate of the High Priest of the Hebrews. Here is the biblical description of the breastplate:

> *And he made the breastplate, artistically woven like the workmanship of the ephod, of gold, blue, purple, and scarlet thread, and of fine woven linen. They made the breastplate square by doubling it; a span was its length and a span its width when doubled. And they set in it four rows of stones: a row with a sardius, a topaz, and an emerald was the first row; the second row, a turquoise, a sapphire, and a diamond; the third row, a jacinth, an agate, and an amethyst; the fourth row, a beryl, an onyx, and a jasper. They were enclosed in settings of gold in their mountings. There were twelve stones according to the names of the sons of Israel: according to their names, engraved like a signet, each one with its own name according to the twelve tribes.*

(NKJV, EXOD. 39:8-14)

These twelve stones from the famous breastplate became linked with the twelve signs of the zodiac, resulting in our cherished modern tradition of birthstones. The long history of birthstones has many more chapters, but an important point to know is that your birthstone is yours by divine right and birthright. I know I was thrilled when I found out amethyst was mine, even though it was ranked as semiprecious. All I knew was that it was purple, my favorite color.

What you need to know about your birthstone is that it is a major power source for you. You should have at least one piece of jewelry made from your birthstone, and treat it as the special stone it is. You should also keep this sacred personal stone around in other forms as well. I have a candleholder made of a large amethyst geode on my mantelpiece surrounded by candles. Just lighting the candle immediately calms and centers me. I realize you can't do that with diamonds, although Herkimer diamonds can be substituted nicely. If you are a January Capricorn, for instance, and your birthstone is garnet, you can have an entire set, or parure, of garnet jewelry—rings, earrings, bracelets, necklaces —for the fullest expression of birthstone power. Surround yourself with your birthstone energy and you will feel at peace, filled with well-being from your gem-fired glow.

Here is the classic list of birthstones by month.

- ✦ JANUARY: **garnet,** a stone symbolizing a light and loyal heart and lasting affection
- ✦ FEBRUARY: **amethyst,** a sexy and sensitive stone; Cleopatra's royal ring
- ✦ MARCH: **aquamarine,** long known as a soothsayer's stone, and **bloodstone,** long known as the martyr's stone
- ✦ APRIL: **diamond,** the traditional engagement ring, which represents the power of love
- ✦ MAY: **emerald,** a lovely green stone of protection
- ✦ JUNE: **pearl, moonstone,** and **alexandrite**—all moon and sea stones powered by water

- JULY: **ruby,** the most highly prized gem of all and a symbol of the essence of life
- AUGUST: **peridot,** the ancient symbol of the sun, and **sardonyx,** an intelligence-enhancing stone
- SEPTEMBER: **sapphire,** a true blue gem that represents the purity of the soul
- OCTOBER: **opal,** said to contain the beauty of all other gems, and **tourmaline,** a stone of inspiration
- NOVEMBER: **topaz,** a stone of royalty, named for the Sanskrit word for fire
- DECEMBER: **turquoise,** which brings luck, and **zircon,** the traveler's stone

## THE BIRTH OF ASTROGEMOLOGY

The ancient art and science of astrology conjoined with crystals comes down to us from 6,000 years ago, when the Sumerians, denizens of the cradle of civilization in Mesopotamia, began marking the metaphysical meanings of the map of the stars. Their neighbors in Ur, the Chaldeans, took this a step further when they observed certain affinities between precious gems and star seasons. At the time, their interests were primarily bounteous crops, bounteous babies, and less plentiful enemies. But the canny Chaldeans were great record-keepers, and they noticed that these recurring patterns tracked with the sky chart and constellations helped them predict what would happen at certain times of the year. Their greatest minds—scholar-scientists, mathematicians, and philosophers—co-created what would become the very dense and deeply meaningful pursuit of astrology. Once they got going, they could predict the

## Tips 'n' Tricks

### BIRTHSTONE BLESSINGS

Sit in a comfortable position with your birthstone placed in a bowl or dish in front of you. Think about the blessings in your life and the gifts your particular stone offers. (To learn more, turn to the descriptionary in Part Two.) What are you grateful for at this moment? There is a powerful magic in recognizing all that you possess and in having an attitude of gratitude. Breathe steadily and deeply, inhaling and exhaling slowly for twenty minutes. As you meditate, send the positive energy into the bowl containing your personal gem.

Now, the birthstone blessings are there anytime you need to access them!

### RINGS OF REJUVENATION

Gemstones and crystals have transformative powers and magic that has been worked with since olden days. Bring birthstone blessings into your life by using these Rings of Rejuvenation.

Sapphire has violet energy. Worn on the first Saturday of the month on the middle finger of the right hand two hours before sunset, the stone is said to be a curative for kidney ailments, epilepsy, tumors, and sciatica.

Diamond, which contains rays of indigo light, is good for maintaining the health of the eyes and nose, managing asthma and laziness, and maintaining sobriety, especially if worn on the right pinkie on Friday during a waxing moon.

Emerald has green light rays and can help with the heart, ulcers, cancer, asthma, and influenza. Wear emerald on the right pinkie on Wednesday two hours after dawn.

Pearls radiate orange rays and operate as a curative if worn on Monday morning by the individual afflicted with insanity, diabetes, colic, or fever.

Topaz has blue rays and helps with laryngitis, paralysis, hysteria, scarlet fever, and assorted glandular disorders if worn on the right ring finger on Thursday mornings.

future, as evidenced by the great biblical story of Jesus Christ's birth and the three kings—astrologers all. Six thousand years ago, learned men were at once priests, doctors, seers, astronomers, and teachers. These special men were also gemologists, cutting, polishing, and, most importantly, studying the gems, rocks, and crystals of their earthly domain. They knew which stones should accompany the dead to the underworld, which rocks portended good fortune if placed over the doorways, and what crystals offered benefits to the body.

The ancient Sumerians had enormous knowledge, for example, about the Dog Star, properly referred to as Sirius A. They knew the density of the star and the length of its orbit (fifty years), and since Sirius A was the brightest star in the night sky, they connected it to the beautiful blue stone they considered to be both powerful and precious—lapis lazuli. They devised a system for assigning colors to the planets, and these associations became the basis for their gem theories:

+ rose and red were connected with the red planet Mars;
+ green was connected with Venus;
+ yellow with the Sun;
+ light blue with Jupiter;
+ blue with Mercury;
+ purple with Saturn; and
+ white with the Moon.

This was just the most basic beginning point for a study that would grow and continue for thousands of years, evolving into today's chemistry, astronomy, and astrology. Without knowing about the big bang theory, the Chaldeans and Sumerians still knew we are all made of the same stuff and came from the same place. We are all interconnected; the minerals from the meteorites that literally fall from the heavens are of the same minerals and elements as our terrestrial rocks. The spectacular process of creation, stemming from the original biggest of bangs, is still happening. Diamonds are the result of millions of years and millions of pounds of pressure on coal, a rather unlovely hunk of earth. The diamonds on our ring fingers started out as coal under our feet. The universe revolves around us in regular cycles, and change is happening at every moment. So, like the clever Chaldeans and the scholarly Sumerians, let us see what we can learn from the stars in the sky and the rocks beneath our feet. Let us learn from patterns, cycles, and connections between the earth and sky.

## The Star of our Solar System

We started out as sun-worshippers on this planet, and the Sun is the center of our planetary system, as Copernicus, my birthday mate (we were both born on February 19), pointed out long ago. Composed of hydrogen and helium, our fantastic and fiery Sun is actually a midsize and rather ordinary star in the whole scheme of things. An impressive 870,331 miles in diameter, the Sun is 300,000 times the size of Earth. Its gravitational pull affects all bodies within a range of nearly 400,000 miles, which is why Earth and all the other planets circle it so loyally. The temperature at the Sun's core has been estimated at seventeen million degrees centigrade, and at its surface, 5,500 degrees.

Astrologically, the Sun is linked with the sign Leo the Lion. Naturally, fire is the element of our Sun. Around old Sol, all the planets rotate, pulled by the gravitational force of the star. Each of the astrological signs and their corresponding stones has a planetary influence.

# SIGNS AND STONES

Each astrological sign is associated with at least one precious gem, or soul stone; one power stone; and one heart stone. The most precious gem for each sign is another kind of birthstone, the jewel marking entry into the world—a guide for your life, if you will. Power stones are lucky omens, and heart stones are the more affordable of crystals, so we can all afford to keep them in our homes, on our desks, and in our bedrooms. I highly recommend them as altar crystals.

## ARIES, *First Half: March 20–April 3*

Pink diamond is the soul stone of choice for early-born Aries. Among the rarest of all diamonds, pink diamonds became a huge fad in late 2002, when actor Ben Affleck gave one to lady love Jennifer Lopez as her engagement ring. They are both Leos, but no matter! Aries babies are ruled by the planet Mars. The finest-quality pink diamonds usually come from Western Australia. A secondary precious-crystal soul stone for this part of Aries is the pink sapphire, also rare.

Sunstone is the power stone for these Aries folks. Appropriately red with an iridescent glow, sunstone is a gold-flecked good-luck charm for the Mars-ruled. Jasper and heliotrope are the other power stones for this part of the year. These red rocks will amp up your lust for life!

The heart stones for these zodiac pioneers are dolomite, rose quartz, and cinnabar. So, Aries, put a rose quartz by your bedside for self-esteem, self-love, and spiritual comfort.

## ARIES, *Last Half: April 4–April 18*

Alexandrite is the designated soul stone here. It is not as rare as pink diamond but is very precious indeed—the scarcest of the chrysoberyls. Usually a dark green, alexandrite shows red under certain types of light. This royal stone is fitting for the first sign of the zodiac. Another soul stone for later-born Aries is rhodonite, a pinkish red crystal that's a favorite of Carl Faberge's.

The power stone for this half of Aries is bowenite, a stone of great strength in a mossy green. While many of the crystals assigned to late Aries are red or pink, this one is green, signifying the other side of the planet Mars. Bowenite is especially precious and sacred to the Maori of New Zealand, where some of the finest specimens come from, and was highly prized by the ancient Indians and Persians. Carnelian is second in line as a power stone and was commonly carved ceremoniously by the Egyptians, the Greeks, and the Phoenicians in the pre-Christian era. Egyptians loved scarabs carved out of the umber-colored chalcedony. Explore the cavalcade of crystal stores on the Internet to find yourself a carnelian carved scarab for a personal power boost.

The heart stone for later-born Aries is the pale pink iridescent stone known as youngite, which looks like a lighter-colored red jasper. One thousand years before Christ, the Egyptians made much jewelry out of this heart stone.

## TAURUS, *First Half: April 19–May 2*

Emerald is the soul stone for those born in the first half of this luxury-loving and Venus-ruled sign. Tauruses are frequently very good with managing wealth and investments, so it makes sense that emeralds are the color of money. If you are an early-born Taurus, you would do well to obtain an emerald and wear it to work and to the bank for enhancing energy.

The power stone for this group is another gorgeous green stone, malachite, which also corresponds to the planet Venus. An earthy rock, it is befitting for this earth sign of the zodiac and has many magical tales to its credit. A malachite heart pendant or paperweight is perfect for early Tauruses.

Pyrite, or fool's gold, is the heart stone for people in this family, who, again, tend to be bankers and money managers. Stunning and shiny, pyrite has a hardness of six, the number sacred to Venus. Pyrite brings great luck to early Tauruses along with abundance and an atmosphere conducive to joy. Delight everyone at work by keeping a chunk of fool's gold on your desk.

## TAURUS, *Second Half: May 3–May 19*

Andalusite is the precious soul stone here, a magically metamorphic crystal. Tauruses are deeply rooted to the earth, and andalusite represents that elemental energy through its range of colors, from earthy black to clear and watery. In fact, andalusite comes in nearly all the colors of the rainbow (yellow, green, red, purple, brown, and gray), manifesting another Venusian quality—glamour.

Jadeite, the power stone for later Tauruses, also comes in many colors. Jadeite is a symbol for abundance and permanence. Jadeite rings with a lovely tone when struck, representing the natural musical talent possessed by members of this sign. A jadeite bracelet, ring, or bowl is essential for the May-born.

Tauruses in this group have a most whimsical heart stone, the Irish fairy stone. This is a mutable crystal made up of several elements: bluish galena, clear quartz crystal, yellow sphalerite, and pyrite. While Irish fairy stone is composed of these different stones, it has its own unique qualities of endurance and stability. This stone brings many blessings to the May Tauruses.

## GEMINI, *First Half: May 20–June 4*

Orange sapphire has long been associated with communication, specifically the telling of truths. As a soul stone, it can help early-half Geminis achieve the mastery of communication that is their karmic due. Sapphires are the hardest gems after diamonds. In India of old, the orange sapphire was prized beyond any other; it was called padparadscha, the Sanskrit word for lotus blossom. The Chaldeans associated this stone with this sign after observing the orange tint of the planet Mercury, the ruler of Gemini.

Moss agate, quartz with a plantlike pattern caused by metallic crystalline grains, is the power stone for first-half Geminis and represents the dualism of this sign of the Twins. The ancients actually thought the dark green markings inside the stone were fossilized moss. They used moss agate for water divining, so it was especially sacred to farmers. It is associated with the metal-rich planet Mercury and makes a great grounding stone for members of this air sign, who need to keep their feet on the ground.

The heart stone for early Geminis is staurolite, named from the Greek word *staurus,* which translates to "cross." Staurolite forms a natural crucifix because of the way the iron molecules in the stone line up. Bright red is one of the colors associated with Geminis, and staurolite most commonly appears in this vibrant color, causing it to be mistaken for garnet. This stone can help Geminis align with their true purpose, so they will benefit from keeping it at their bedsides or on their desks.

## GEMINI, *Second Half: June 5–June 20*

Cat's-eye, the lovely golden yellow gem, is the special soul stone for late-born Geminis. The ancient Greeks, who called this crystal cymophane, meaning "waving light," believed this stone guarded against danger to the soul and the body. The iridescent surface of the stone causes it to appear in different colors; the shade depends on the angle from which the cat's-eye is being seen. This mutable stone reflects back to Geminis their changeable nature and helps them to acknowledge their quicksilver personalities and to grow from that deep recognition. Geminis, wear a cat's-eye ring and see your soul reflected back at you.

Late Geminis can count on the garnet known as Transvaal jade, or grossular, for their power. People most often think of garnets as red stones of great clarity, but this specimen is opaque and a beautiful bright green. Under certain light, it appears as a blazing yellow color. This ability to change color symbolizes the dual nature of the June-born. Originating many millions of years ago in the deep core of the earth, Transvaal jade contains many metals in its makeup, a fact that also corresponds to the Gemini nature of having so many different qualities and talents. Wearing this garnet can awaken hidden talents in Geminis and bring them to the fore.

Geode, which usually comes in two split halves, is the ideal heart stone for later-born Geminis, but they must have both halves to help integrate the two parts of their nature and make for a complete, whole person. Geodes are formed from old volcanic bubbles and are usually solid agate outside with a center of gorgeous amethyst, opal, or rock crystal. If you are a Gemini, I recommend keeping one of the geode halves at home on your altar or in a special spot where you can see it every day and the other half at your place of work, to reflect and connect the two parts of your nature.

## Tips 'n' Tricks

### TWIN HEARTS

Many crystal shops and New Age stores now feature heart-shaped rocks. The next time you see heart-shaped amethyst crystals, buy two right away and give one to your true love. The gift of an amethyst heart will ensure a happy life together and good fortune shared. Sweet!

## CANCER, *First Half: June 21–July 4*

Cancers are ruled by the Moon, so it is appropriate that moonstone is the precious soul stone for individuals born in the first half of this sign. The most priceless of moonstones is adularia, named after the place it was first discovered —Adula, Switzerland. Moonstones have an opalescent sheen reminiscent of the Moon in the night sky. Adularia was special to early Europeans who believed it could improve the memory, help stop seizures, overcome a broken heart, and foretell the future. Wearing moonstone jewelry will put Cancers in tune with their lunar-influenced changeable natures, giving them strength and the wisdom of intuition.

Pearl is the power stone of great price for early Cancers. Pearls have a long and rich history; they were first written about in China 4,000 years ago and were celebrated in all the ancient cultures of the world after humankind first opened a shell and found the prize inside. Cancers are the great historians of the zodiac, and they have incredible memories. They are connected to pearls because of a common link with the ocean and the tides, which are regulated by Cancer's ruler, the Moon. If you are a Cancer, honor your native element, water, by wearing pearls on occasion, but not constantly, and by decorating your home and work space with shells. This will help you stay secure, refreshed, and relaxed and help you avoid your great nemesis—worry.

Calcite, made up of many fossilized seashells, is the heart stone for first-half Cancers. Because the ocean makes up so much of the surface of the planet (and encompassed even more area in the first few million of Earth's years), calcite is common, but there are many lovely specimens, such as Iceland spar, flos ferri, and nailhead calcite. Iceland spar is a beautiful clear type of calcite, and when you look at it from certain angles you can see a double image. Nailhead calcite shows many small, rounded circles of variegated colors. Flos ferri, maybe the most beautiful of the three calcite stones, boasts fragile, white, treelike branches that take on other colors when exposed to different minerals. Cancers, scatter this Moon-ruled rock all around your homes for grounding and healing.

## CANCER, *Second Half: July 5–July 21*

Opal is the soul stone for later-born Cancers. Opals can't be duplicated artificially due to the complicated nature of their patterning, varying hues, and play of color. The most precious of all opals feature a star, called an asterism. Opals are mysterious, just like Cancers, having much depth beneath their protective shells. The ancients exulted about opals; Pliny the Elder wrote, "For in them you shall see the living fire of ruby, the glorious purple of the amethyst, the sea-green of the emerald, all glittering together in an incredible mixture of light." Cancer, you will come into your true soul's purpose by wearing opal jewelry.

Red coral is the power stone for the second half of Cancer. It is formed by lime secreted by sea creatures to create their homes. One memorable old story associated with the oceanic gem is the ancient Greek belief that sea sprites stole Medusa's severed head and took it to the bottom of the sea, and that each drop of her blood formed a red coral. The stone was believed to be healing and protective then, and it still is today. For Cancers, red coral is good for vitality and is a symbol of life and love and health. Wear red coral beads over your heart and you will immediately feel vibrant.

Desert rose, formed of cemented sand particles, is the heart stone for this group of Cancers. The Saharan Bedouin believed it was formed from the tears of women mourning for those who died in battle. Desert rose is gypsum originating in lake bottoms that have become desert and comes in beautiful earth tones of red, yellow, gray, brown, and pink. For later Cancers, this heart stone helps contain and release emotions in a healthy, expressive way. Decorate your bedroom, your inner sanctum, with desert rose for a soothing and calming effect.

## LEO, *First Half: July 22–August 5*

Yellow diamond is a brilliant soul stone, befitting the king of the zodiacal wheel. Diamond is pure carbon and the hardest substance on Earth, and its name appropriately originates from the Greek word *adamas,* meaning "invincible." Yellow diamonds represent the Sun, the ruling planet for Leos and the symbol of this sign's high level of consciousness—true heart, great generosity, and incredible courage. Yellow diamond earrings will keep you Leos in balance.

First-half Leos can count zircon as their power stone. Beloved by early cultures, the brilliant zircon was believed to be a safeguard against poison and was thought to be a holy healer in India. In the early Roman Catholic church, it was held to be the sign of humility. For Leos, whose downfall can be pride, zircon can guard against this and keep the astrological Lions on an even keel.

Early-born Leos have a special heart stone in lesser-known vandanite, which can be a beautiful red orange or a glorious yellow gold. Vandanite is rich in lead and also vanadium, the mineral used to strengthen steel. Vandanite is formed at intense temperatures, which can be related to our Sun, a furnace in the heavens. For Leos, this unusual heart stone can help them deal with the pressure of a lot of attention, which Leos naturally attract with their vibrant and magnetic personalities. You should keep your heart stone at home and at work for optimum stability and inspiration.

## LEO, *Second Half: August 6–August 21*

White diamond is the soul gem for late Leos. It is regarded as the purest of all of the hard, pure-carbon crystals. Old cultures deemed this diamond a guard against harm and a bringer of great fortune and enlightenment. Gemologists sometimes refer to this stone as "of the first water," in reference to its unmatched purity. The lion is the king of the beasts, and Leo the Lion is zodiacal royalty; white diamond is as hot as the Sun itself. Leos can use this rock in all jewelry to aspire to the greatness within it.

Heliodor, named for Helios, the Greek god of the sun, is the ultimate power stone for second-half Leos. Heliodor, a member of the beryl family, is the sunny yellow sister of the popular green emerald and blue aquamarine. It is formed under extremely high temperatures and pressures. Heliodor can help you Leos call upon your greatest qualities and talents and provide the impetus to go out and try to make your dreams come true!

The heart stone for later-born Leos is most unexpected—sulfur, called brimstone in biblical times. Sulfur is a very dynamic rock; the crystals enlarge even by the heat of a hand that holds it. If you rub sulfur, it will give off a negative charge. A cluster of sulfur is a luminous mass of gold crystals and is quite beautiful despite the images its name may conjure. Obviously, sulfur is associated with fire and has been used for centuries in explosive materials such as gunpowder, fireworks, and matches. Leo is a fire sign, and Leos can hold emotions in until they ignite and explode. Keeping sulfur at home can help Leos stay balanced and release their energy in healthy and positive ways.

## VIRGO, *First Half: August 22–September 5*

Black opal is the soul stone for early Virgos. Virgos are perhaps the most discriminating of signs and would relish the fact that until recently, black opals came from only a few acres in Australia. The ancient Romans, seeing the rainbow colors of opals, believed them to be the bridge between heaven and Earth, but they especially desired the few poor-quality black opals (now believed to have been faked) held by the barbarians in Hungary. The finest grade of black opal was discovered on the island of Java, in Indonesia. For Virgos, only the best and only the real black opals will do. Members of the sign of service and help to others, Virgos gain strength and intensity and augment their own purity with black opals. This stone has been called the gem of hope, and, as such, offers a high level of consciousness for Virgos.

The power talisman for first-half Virgos is labradorite, the lovely iridescent stone that originated in Labrador. Like Geminis, Virgos are ruled by Mercury, and the quicksilver, peacock-hued labradorite is good for providing the mental swiftness Virgos need to accomplish all of their goals in life. This type of feldspar can reflect every color of the spectrum and helps Virgos from becoming too task oriented—too focused on one thing. No one can work harder than Virgos, and labradorite can prevent exhaustion from overwork and can also ensure that early Virgos activate a variety of talents.

Magnetite, also known as lodestone, is the optimal heart stone for first-half Virgos. Another glittery, surface-changing rock, magnetite contains a lot of iron, and thanks to its common occurrence and adaptability, it is popular in jewelry. Virgos are associated with health, medicine, and nursing, and magnetite has become a good healing stone because of its magnetic qualities. If you are a Virgo, wear this stone and give it to people you love for good health and prosperity.

## VIRGO, *Second Half: September 6–September 21*

Virgos in this group celebrate iolite as their precious soul gem, which is associated with their ruling planet Mercury due to its crystalline composition of two dark and two light metallic elements. Iolite is named after the Greek word *ios,* meaning "violet." Formed under enormous pressure in extremely high temperatures, iolite has a high vibration. The stone can help Virgos stay out of career ruts and achieve their true spiritual natures.

Tiger's-eye, another iridescent gem, is the power stone for later Virgos, denoting strength and courage and perception. Virgos are great critics, missing no flaw, and tiger's-eye can help them to have incredible vision and be able to see the wonderful possibilities in all things.

The heart stone for second-half Virgos is obsidian, a glinting black, extremely hard and tough natural glass formed by volcanic activity. Virgos are always helping other people and sometimes become vulnerable because of this. Using obsidian as home decoration can help them keep all of their energy from going to others and causing imbalance. Some obsidians have stripes; in ancient Mexico, where obsidian was plentiful, the striped variety was believed to prevent negative, or dark, magic. Virgos can be extremely self-critical, and having obsidian nearby can absorb their negativity and help turn it positive. This is an essential stone for the September-born!

## LIBRA, *First Half: September 22–October 6*

A soul stone that was extremely popular in days of old is spinel, a jewel available in a multitude of hues, including black, dark green, orange, white, blue, purple, and red. Spinels were symbols and stones of the royals; the Queen of England owns a grand specimen called the Timur ruby, and the czars of Russia wore a crown decorated with a magnificent spinel. Spinels are rarer than either rubies or sapphires, and I predict they will have a renaissance. The extremely rare and precious green spinel is the type most highly prized among Libras, and it can bring out their aesthetic values and empower their pursuit of the arts.

Dioptase is the power stone for first-half Libras. A deeper green than any emerald, it has an extensive copper content. Venus is associated with the color green, and the intensity of this gorgeous green stone makes it a love crystal for Venus-ruled Libras, enriching both their personal relationships and their higher love for humankind. Dioptase can also awaken the spiritual side of Libras, making the usually attractive members of this sign even more beautiful inside and out. Dioptase is difficult to cut for jewelry because of its brittleness. Use uncut crystal clusters as lovely spirit enhancers all around the home.

Kyanite is the sky-colored heart stone for early Libras. Because it shares the same chemistry (but different crystal structure) as a couple of other minerals, kyanite is known as a stone of symmetry, perfect for providing balance. The Greeks favored this aluminum-based rock and called it disthene, meaning "dual strength," because it is soft (and easily cut) lengthwise but much harder across. Kyanite most commonly occurs in long, bluish green crystal blades but also comes in clustered rosettes with a pearly, opalescent surface. If you're a Libra, an air sign, keep kyanite around to stay steady and strong and help avoid spreading yourself too thin and succumbing to petty, energy-draining distractions.

## LIBRA, *Second Half: October 7–October 22*

Blue sapphire, exceedingly rare and of exceptionally high quality, is the soul gem of choice for later-born Libras. The name "sapphire" has several origins, among them *sapphirus,* the Latin word for blue. The blue in the stone comes from the iron and titanium inside. This gem represents Venus's glinting blue in the blue black of the darkened heavens. Libras are great romantics, and blue sapphire's high vibration of love can activate their creativity so they can craft great works of art—songs, poetry, paintings, and anything their imaginations can conceive.

The power talisman for this group of Libras is jadeite, sometimes called imperial green jade. The Chinese highly prize this stone in their lengthy history and culture and believe it contains all that you need for a happy, long life—courage, modesty, charity, wisdom, and, most important for the Libra scales to be in balance, justice. Jade bookends on your desk are perfect balancers.

Limonite, an icicle-like mineral appearing in long, shiny pieces, is the heart stone for second-half Libras. This represents the striving for higher mind, higher beauty, and higher love necessary for the completion of Libra karma.

## SCORPIO, *First Half: October 23–November 6*

The soul stone for early Scorpios is ruby, a gem celebrated in many legends dating from prehistoric times to the present day. Rubies were believed to be dragons' eggs—very fitting for Scorpios, who have a lizard aspect to their souls. Rubies were believed to give the wearers invincibility. They were also thought to warn of danger by darkening in shade to a red that was nearly black. Rubies correspond to Mars, the first ruling planet of Scorpio, also associated with red. The most valuable rubies outrank even diamonds, and in the Bible, ruby is called the most precious of the gems first created in the world. If worn by a Scorpio, a ruby can rechannel passions such as lust, jealousy, and anger into more positive emotions. By all means, wear rubies, soulful Scorpios!

First-half Scorpios have a most unusual power stone in blue John. It is found in only one place in the world: the underground caverns beneath a hill in the county of Derbyshire, England. The Roman emperor Nero was crazy for it and paid an enormous price for a single vase made from it. It is the rarest of the fluorites, and its appearance of dark blue and reddish purple bands on a white background relates to Pluto, the second ruling planet of Scorpio. Scorpio is the sign of the underworld and of secrets, and the origin of the name of its talisman is a mystery no one has yet solved. Though blue John can be difficult to come by, other fluorites are more readily available and will substitute nicely for the rare stone. Fluorite is thought to be healing to the bones and to wounds that lie underneath the surface. Secretive Scorpios carry many hurts beneath strong exteriors, and fluorite can gently resolve these over time.

For early Scorpios, the heart stone is stibnite, a blue-gray mineral that comes in clusters of needle-like rods. Stibnite is closely associated with Pluto and has a shiny and opalescent surface. It is soft, and because of its crumbliness, stibnite is very difficult to form into jewelry, which is why it is not more commonly known. Scorpios can be so intense that they can become hard, and stibnite greatly alleviates this, making it easier for Scorpios to get along with other people and get along better in the world. If you're a Scorpio, you know you have a strong will; this stone can help you get your ideas across without forcing them. A chunk of stibnite on your desk at work will help your career and reputation.

## *Tips 'n' Tricks*

### STONES FOR SUCCESS

It is no accident that this guide to achievement is placed in the area of ambitious Capricorn. However, these stones for paving the path to prosperity are for everyone:

- **Azurite** strengthens mental powers.
- **Chalcedony** gives you get-up-and-go!
- **Emerald** aids in problem solving.
- **Opal** encourages faithful service.
- **Pearl** engenders material wealth.
- **Quartz** helps overcome fear of rejection.
- **Sapphire** helps with goal setting.
- **Tourmaline** promotes an attitude of accomplishment.

## SCORPIO, *Second Half: November 7–November 21*

Rhodochrosite is the precious soul stone for later Scorpios. Once called rosinca, or Inca rose, this pink beauty takes its color from iron, magnesium, and calcium. Rhodochrosite corresponds to the planets Mars, Pluto, and the Moon. The gem is formed over a very long period of time under relatively gentle geological circumstances and therefore has a gentle energy that calms the volcanic passions and anger that commonly erupt in Scorpios. As mentioned previously, Scorpios carry so much under the surface in silence. This gem can enable you to express your feelings healthily.

Everybody thinks of amethyst as the February crystal for Aquarians and Pisceans, but it is also the power stone for second-half Scorpios. The purple color relates to the purple planet, Pluto. Amethyst can open the love vibration for individuals ruled by this most misunderstood and enormously powerful water sign. Wearing amethyst jewelry and keeping chunks of amethyst crystal in the home and workplace can reveal the sweet, funny, smart, approachable, and lovable side of Scorpios, offering them a much greater chance for happiness.

Scorpios have for their heart stone the very available quartz crystal. Quartz is a tremendous healer, and so are Scorpios, though they rarely receive credit for this latent talent. When a Scorpio puts her mind to something, nothing can stand in the way! By acknowledging and utilizing the healing power of quartz crystal, Scorpios can use their personal power for the good of others and greatly benefit. Surround yourself with this inexpensive heat crystal and feel the love.

## SAGITTARIUS, *First Half: November 22–December 5*

Tourmaline—specifically the multihued specimen known as melonstone, which is pinkish red with a blue-green stripe—is the precious soul stone for the Jupiter-ruled Sagittarians. Individuals under this fire sign are lively and very action-oriented, and tourmaline, which readily gives off an electrical charge when warmed, can match and propel their energy. Tourmaline is the stone for adventurers and explorers. Get some today and hit the road, dear Sag.

Amber is the power stone for early Sagittarians. This rock formed from fossilized tree sap and resin, an organic crystal. Amber was thought by the ancients to have trapped the sun, and it was called electron by the Greeks, who observed its negative electrical charge. Even wildly active Sagittarians should wear this stone only on special occasions. It keeps energy cycling within, which is good, but it can have a weakening effect if worn all the time. Amber helps performers; actors and musicians swear by it.

Chrysocolla is the heart stone for first-half Sagittarians. Either blue or green, this copper-rich crystal is one of great life-giving vibrancy. Sagittarians always have many irons in many fires and often burn up their energy in typical fire-sign style. Chrysocolla can help prevent this and help Sagittarians direct their energy toward more purposeful and heartfelt pursuits.

## SAGITTARIUS, *Second Half: December 6–December 20*

Tourmaline is also the soul stone for later-born Sagittarians. (See "Sagittarius, First Half," above.)

Turquoise is this group's power stone. The rock has a rich and colorful history and was valued in the extreme by the Persians, Egyptians, Mexicans, Bedouin, Chinese, Tibetans, Native Americans, and Turks. Turquoise is associated with horses and riders; Sagittarius is the centaur of the zodiac—half man and half horse. Once revered as the eye of Ra, the Egyptian sun-god, turquoise lends sight and aids in travel. Wearing this stone will help people born in this part of the year to find their purpose and harness the passion and vision to see it through.

The heart stone for second-half Sagittarians is bornite, a burnished red rock of copper and iron. Bornite used to be called peacock ore because of its impressive iridescent coloration. It is a very powerful energy crystal. Although it is not widely known, Sagittarians can be indecisive, and this stone abets them in overcoming that. This is also a stone of justice; Jupiter-ruled Sagittarians are lovers of justice.

## CAPRICORN, *First Half: December 21–January 6*

Topaz in any of its color incarnations is the soul stone for early Capricorns. Topaz gained its name from sailors who found it while exploring the desert island upon which they were shipwrecked. They named both the stone and the island Topazos, translating to mean "lost and then found." With topaz, ambitious Capricorns will leave no stone unturned in the path to glory.

For power stones, first-half Goats have both lazulite and jet, gems that have a dark and shadowy appearance representative of Saturn, Capricorn's ruling planet. Jet is one of the oldest stones known to man, fitting with the longevity of the slow and steady Capricorns, reputed to grow more youthful as they get older. Wear jet to live long and prosper!

Citrine and smoky quartz are the heart stones for this sector of the zodiac and will ground this hardworking earth sign. Keep citrine at your place of work and wear citrine rings and necklaces frequently to remain in touch with your feelings.

## CAPRICORN, *Second Half: January 7–January 19*

Tanzanite is the sacred soul stone for these Capricorns. A gorgeous purple stone found in 1967 in Tanzania, it corresponds to the ruling planet of Saturn. Appropriately regal and rare, it is as serious as the sign it signifies. For important meetings and moments in your life, a tanzanite jewel will make you a shining star!

Lucky Goats in the latter half of Capricorn get to have lapis lazuli as their talismanic power crystal. This crystal was absolutely revered by the Egyptians and other Mesopotamian cultures. A bright blue, this stone connotes wisdom, accomplishment, and value. I highly suggest lots of lapis boxes, jewelry, and figurines for full esteem ahead.

Rock crystal is a most practical heart stone for these Capricorns. Known as the salt of the earth, this form of quartz is fairly common but is also perhaps the single most effective and most often used stone in magic. I have been seeing rock crystal lamps that give a beautiful glow and pleasurable negative ions. Decorate with these lamps and you'll go far and feel good with the process.

## AQUARIUS, *First Half: January 20–February 3*

Olivine is the soul gem of choice for first-half Aquarians, and it is a stone with a royal heritage. The Egyptians believed this peridot to be a stone of the gods. The long, convoluted, and quite bizarre history of this stone entirely suits Aquarians, who are ruled by Uranus, the planet of chaos and unexpected change. Wear a dark green olivine on momentous occasions to mark them as special in your life.

Onyx, the deep, dark power stone for early Aquarians, was beloved by peoples of prehistory and by craftsmen of the classical era. Onyx is super for grounding you airy Aquarians!

The heart stone for this group is moldavite. With its otherworldly origin as a meteorite, it is perfect for the Uranian bolt-from-the-blue these scientist-philosophers represent. Moldavite is a mysterious and powerful crystal with many mist-shrouded legends and theories. No doubt, an Aquarius will get to the bottom of them all one day. Moldavite will add to your Aquarian brilliance and boost your personal creativity to new heights.

## AQUARIUS, *Second Half: February 4–February 18*

Diopside is the beautiful blue soul stone for later-born Aquarians. This stone has ties to both Uranus, the official ruling planet of Aquarius, and Saturn, the sign's ruler before Uranus was discovered. In 1964, star diopside, an included type, was found; it is a magical and stunningly gorgeous stone that has a quality of electric enlightenment, just like these February-born inventors, artists, and visionary businesspeople.

Late Aquarians have jade for a power stone. It is a universal healer and love stone that can keep these very intellectually oriented people in touch with their hearts and bodies.

The heart stone for second-half Aquarians is charoite, a purple mineral that corresponds with Venus, Saturn, and Uranus. This is a fairly recent rock, perfect for the modern-minded February-born, who are generally fifty years ahead of everyone else. Charoite was discovered circa 1947 near the Chara River in Russia and was immediately greeted as a very special stone for the new centuries.

## PISCES, *First Half: February 19–March 4*

I have a vested interest in the gem lore regarding Pisces as my birthday is February 19! The sign of the Fishes is affected by the moons of three different planets: Triton, Neptune's largest moon; Io, one of Jupiter's moons; and our moon here on Earth. Because Pisces is represented by a pair of fish, members of the first half of this sign share two different soul stones. The first is the oceanic blue-green diamond, associated with Neptune, the ruling planet of Pisces. Aquamarine, which relates to all three of the aforementioned moons, is the second soul gem for the Fishes. Aquamarine was once believed to be the dried tears of sea nymphs. It is the purest, most harmonious energy-enhancing stone for Pisceans; wear it and you will stay in the swim.

For their power talisman, early Pisceans have a mutable rock, smithsonite, a soft, calcium-based stone that comes in a variety of lovely pastel colors. It is a stone for creativity, the bailiwick of this sign. Keep smithsonite at your easel, drawing table, or writing desk.

Opal fossils, the heart stones for these sensitive people, are ancient fragments that crystallized and achieved iridescence through an accumulation of water and minerals over time. Pisces is, of course, a water sign and is also associated with history and deep, old wisdom.

## PISCES, *Second Half: March 5–March 19*

The soul gem for the very end of the zodiac is kunzite, a very lovely lilac-rose-colored stone that was discovered at the very beginning of the twentieth century, about one minute ago in geological terms. Before the planet Neptune was discovered, Pisces shared its former ruling planet, Jupiter, with Sagittarius; kunzite is a *Jovian* (relating to Jupiter) gem. It is a sensitive stone, which befits a sensitive people. Kunzite will help you face this pressure-filled world and stay above the fray with grace.

The power stone for late Pisces is chrysoprase, a gem that has been revered through the ages. Chrysoprase was assigned sovereignty and utilized by high priests of nearly every era. This crystal is perfect for the sign that can attain the highest level of spiritual evolution. With chrysoprase, you can help others and yourself through soul attunement.

Late Pisceans can count as their heart stone the all-purpose fluorite, which comes in a rainbow of colors corresponding to the rainbow gills of fish. This stone is found all over our planet and is so universally helpful that it presents a solid foundation for gentle Pisceans. Fluorite at home and work will add comfort and grace to your space.

# BEDAZZLING BIRTHSTONES

For centuries, gemstones have been assigned as symbols of image and identity. Countries have national gems. The signs of the zodiac and the twelve months of the year, as we know, have special stone correspondences, as do the planets. These systems were established long ago by the earliest astronomers and scientists. Even the twelve apostles had special stones assigned to them with sacred meanings! The very gates of heaven are covered in precious gems, according to lore and religious rites. According to the Bible, God's own throne is made of red jasper.

Birthstones carry a long and cherished history and tradition, and you contain your stone's energy through your right of birth. See how you can bring more of that birthstone magic into your life. For example, if you are an Aquarius, wear your garnet birthstone to help put you more in touch with your emotions and enhance your relationships at home and at work. If you are a typical travel-happy Sagittarius, now you know your birthstone is specially equipped to protect you when you are far away from home. For romantic Libra women, your opal is a "man magnet."

Study up! Aside from adding sparkle to your appearance, your birthstone is surrounding you with magic that you can access to your advantage each and every day. If you don't have one, think about giving yourself your special and sacred birthstone as a birthday gift!

*Chapter Four*

# CRYSTAL
# POWER

You have begun to explore the potency of gems and crystals and how they can come to your aid in many ways, large and small. Through the blessings of birthstones and some supernatural self-help in imbuing your jewelry with supportive magic, you are discovering the amazing world of natural gems and crystals. Now, we will come to know the deep power these stones have to calm and center you, reveal wisdom, and strengthen your body, spirit, and soul. The possibilities of crystal power are truly limitless once you begin tapping into the wisdom of the stones and using them as tools to take your life in the directions you hope for and dream of.

Ancient cultures used gem and stone beads in everyday practices to enhance their quality of life. While these early peoples used crystals for ceremonies and to ornament themselves, they knew instinctively that there was a spirit in each stone. Respectfully, they used gems as tools and talismans to symbolize their tribes and help them give birth, accumulate wealth, and create art. Stones were an important part of society from the very beginning, and they remain so today. In fact, the royal houses of the world are identified as such by precious crown jewels. Today, you can use crystals and gems for getting a job, improving relationships, and growing as a person. We'll begin with crystal energy exercises, and then you will learn to create for yourself tools and talismans for manifesting magical change in your life.

## ON THE RISE WITH ROSE

If you want to jump-start your life and bring about positive change, tap into the power of the rose and red stones. Stones of this side of the color spectrum contain life's energy and can help you become more motivated, more energetic, and more vibrant, and also give you an appealing aura. Wear this list of rosy and red stones or place them on your desk and throughout your home for an instant boost: alexandrite, carnelian, garnet, red coral, red jasper, rhyolite, rose jasper, and ruby.

# ENERGY MANAGEMENT—
# YOU AND YOUR CRYSTALS

The first thing you need to do with a crystal is to *charge* it, which means syncing it up with your personal frequency and vibrations. You're placing your desires and wishes into the vessel of the crystal. The crystal's inherent energies will come into play with your personal power, and your intentions can be manifested, or made real, through the crystal.

The very first step in this process, however, is the dedication of the crystal toward the greater good of all beings. An essential part of this process is the cleansing of the crystal in order to purify its energy. Although this is a straight-forward task, it is of supreme importance for your use of the crystal down the road. If a gem or stone is not as effective as you had hoped, the problem could stem from the initial dedication. Think of this primary step as the honing and direction of the intention. Here is how: Simply hold the crystal in the palm of your right hand, and in your mind picture a glow of light surrounding the stone.

When the rock is completely enveloped by light in your mind's eye, state out loud, "This crystal is only for exacting good of the highest order. In this stone of the earth, there is only love and light." I like to leave the crystal out in the light of the natural orbs of the sun and the moon for a twenty-four-hour period for the maximum dedication of light and love from the universe and the heavens above as part of the purification process. But, if time is of the essence, you can move right on to step number two, charging the crystal itself.

All stones possess natural energies of their very own. You want to merge your energies with those of your crystals so that the crystals will be in sync with your vibratory channel. Remain mindful of the great power your stones have and you will be in a good position to work with it. Consider carefully what kind of energy you want to place into your crystal. Take a stone that has been cleansed by sitting in a bowl of sea salt overnight and in the light of the sun for a day. Sit in a comfortable position and hold the crystal in your right hand. Focus on the energy you desire your crystal to hold and project it into the stone. Bear in mind, the use of gem magic should not be used solely for your purposes, but also for the greater good. Please make sure you're projecting positive energy and not anger or hatred. You should ask aloud for your crystal to work together with you for the highest good. You are doing creative visualization here, so keep concentrating until you can see and feel the energy flowing into the stone. You will feel when the charging, or programming, is complete; your intuition will tell you.

While it is not the best-case scenario, you can charge a stone for someone else. For example, if you have a friend who is very ill and halfway around the world, you could charge the crystal with positive, healing energy and send it to your friend to help him. Ask the crystal to work for the highest good of this person and then release that crystal to him.

# Tools of the Magic Trade

With gem magic, you can make your own ritual accessories and tools as you wish. Your intentions and personal energy are the driving forces behind the enchantments you create. For many people, their most important tool is the wand, but don't be afraid to experiment with new mystical implements. You'll be amazed as the various crystal accoutrements hold and collect the energy of all your magical workings and your power grows.

## *Wonderful Wands*

I see many gorgeous, crystal-encrusted wands for sale in metaphysical five-and-dimes, and I am sure they are superpowered. Bear in mind, though, that it is a wonderful thing indeed to make your own wand. Start with a tree branch that has fallen to the ground on its own. Sand and polish the rough edges, as it is a wand and not a weapon. Then give it a good smudging. Hot-glue a large quartz crystal onto the wand near the handle, and hot-glue on any crystals featuring properties that will complement your magic. Citrine makes an excellent pointer tip for your wand and aligns your self-identity with your spirit. And, after all, isn't that the point? Here are stones I recommend for harnessing various powers with wands:

+ **amber** for grounding,
+ **amethyst** for balance and intuition,
+ **aventurine** for creative visualization,
+ **bloodstone** for abundance and prosperity,
+ **calcite** for warding off negativity,
+ **carnelian** for opening doors for you and helping you overcome any family problems,

- **chalcedony** for power over dark spirits,
- **citrine** for getting motivated and attracting money and success,
- **fluorite** for communicating with fairies and other unseen beings,
- **garnet** for protection from gossip,
- **geode** for getting through periods of extreme difficulty,
- **hematite** for strength and courage,
- **jade** for wisdom to interpret or realize powerful dreams,
- **jasper** for stability,
- **lodestone** for bringing a lover back into your life,
- **mahogany obsidian** for feeling sexy and emanating sensuality,
- **moss agate** for powers of persuasion and healing,
- **quartz crystal** for divining your dreams,
- **rhodochrosite** for staying on course with your life's true purpose,
- **rose quartz** for love,
- **turquoise** for safety when traveling, and
- **watermelon tourmaline** for help with planning your best possible future.

## Pendulums

The pendulum is a tool for gleaning information from your inner self. Some of the best pendulums are the ones you can make yourself by tying a piece of string or rawhide to a crystal. You should tie it so that the crystal points down. Each time you use it, ask the pendulum, "Show me yes or show me no." The crystal pendulum will swing up and down, giving you answers. I recommend keeping a journal of your work with the pendulum. Not only will this give you a record of the yes-and-no responses, but it will also help you track their effectiveness, and you will be able to see patterns of information emerging from your unconscious and the universe. I can't recommend this highly enough. You will learn so much about yourself and your place in the world from this. I know people who absolutely depend on their pendulums for help with shopping and all manner of decision making.

Most New Age shops now sell lovely chunks of amethyst and quartz attached to delicate chains. Do try this easiest of all forms of divination. It is fun and full of surprises!

## Rune Stones

Moonstone is reputed to be the most powerful crystal for use in rune stones, the tools used for a specialized form of divination. *Runes,* or letters from a language used by early Nordic peoples, are carved into the stones and are said to hone and intensify the intuition of the reader divining the future from them. You, too, can use a bag of lustrous and mysterious moonstones to get in touch with your powers of perception. While others throw the I Ching or read their horoscopes with their morning coffee, you can pull a rune and contemplate its meaning for your day.

## Amulets

The term "amulet" comes from the Latin word meaning "defense." Indeed, amulets are a way to protect yourself that dates back from the earliest human beliefs. Pliny himself subscribed to the use of amulets and wrote about three common kinds used by the Romans of the classical age. A typical amulet of that era was a bit of parchment inscribed with protective words, rolled up in a metal cylinder, and worn around the neck. Evil eyes might be the most global of all amulets, the belief being that they could ward off a hex by simply reflecting it back to its origins. Phallic symbols have always been popular, too, coming in the shapes of horns, hands, and the phallus, of course. Some amulets were devoted to a specific god or goddess, and the wearer of such a piece would be protected by that divine entity.

The peoples of the Mesopotamian plain wore amulets. The Assyrians and Babylonians favored cylindrical seals encrusted with precious stones. They also loved animal talismans for the qualities associated with different animals: lions for courage, bulls for virility, and so on. The ancient Egyptians absolutely depended on their amulets for use in burial displays, and we can see many preserved in the cases of today's museums. To make their amulets, the Egyptians employed a material called faience, a glazed composition of ground quartz that was typically blue green in color. Wealthier denizens of the Nile, royalty, and the priestly class wore precious and semiprecious gems and crystals as amulets. Lapis lazuli was perhaps the most revered of these and was worn in many shapes, the eye of Horus being the most significant religious icon, followed by the scarab, symbolizing rebirth; the frog, symbolizing fertility; and the ankh, representing eternal life.

Organized religions appropriated the idea of amulets from pagan peoples, and it was very popular in medieval times to wear a tiny verse from the Torah, the Bible, or the Koran. Today, many a Catholic wears a medal honoring a given saint, such as Saint Christopher, the patron saint for travelers. Wiccans and modern pagans are great proponents of protective amulets, causing a resurgence in Celtic symbols and imagery.

Amulets are very easy to create and make nice gifts, as long as you believe your friends will truly benefit from them and are aware of the special qualities and powers they hold. To make one, select a crystal that is endowed with the desired energy. Hold it in the palm of your hand until it is warm from your touch. Then, visualize the specific power the stone is offering. If you're giving your amulet to yourself, wear it as a pendant or tuck it into your pocket or purse for a "guardian to go." Here is a list of stones from which to choose for the specific kind of safeguard you are in need of:

+ **Amethyst** helps with sobriety by preventing inebriation.
+ **Aquamarine** is good for attracting wisdom and overcoming a fear of water and drowning. It is also a guard against malevolent spirits.
+ **Bloodstone** brings luck and is good to wear during travels.
+ **Carnelian** is to the devil as garlic is to a vampire—keeps him away!
+ **Chrysolite** drives away evil spirits and promotes peaceful sleep, especially if set in gold.
+ **Diamond** in a necklace brings good fortune and lends force and valor. This dazzling stone should always touch the skin and works best when it is received as a gift.
+ **Emerald** can cancel out the power of any magician!
+ **Jade** offers protection, especially for children, and guards their health. It also creates prosperity.
+ **Jasper** is reputed to be a defense against the venom of poisonous insects and snakes.
+ **Jet** set in silver will help expel negativity.
+ **Moonstone** is another boon to travelers and brings fortune and fame.
+ **Turquoise** is believed to be great for a horse's gait if affixed to the animal's bridle.

## Talismans

A talisman is a decorative object, or *objet,* that also provides protection and has magical properties. A talisman can be any article or symbol that you believe has mystical qualities. As we know, many gems and crystals have special innate powers. With a talisman, the special powers can be naturally present or instilled during a ritual. People often confuse amulets with talismans, but they differ in this significant way: Amulets *passively protect* the wearer from harm, evil, and negativity. Talismans *actively transform* the wearer to have certain powers. For example, the supernatural sword Excalibur, imbued with supremacy by the Lady of the Lake, gave King Arthur magical powers.

Grimoires (spell books) offer instruction on making talismans. The reasons for using talismans are many—for love, for wealth, for luck with gambling, for the gift of a silver tongue, for a good memory, for the prevention of death. Whatever you can think of, there is probably a talisman for that exact purpose!

## Sacred Stone Shapes

+ **Ankh**-shaped stones represent the key to life. Use this ancient Egyptian symbol to develop creativity, wisdom, and fertility.

+ **Clusters** are among the most common natural crystal forms and bring balance and harmony into your life.

+ **Diamond**-shaped stones bring the energy of wealth and abundance and are said to attract riches.

+ **Egg**-shaped stones denote creativity and give new ideas to anyone wearing them.

+ **Heart**-shaped stones are love energy. They promote self-love and romance.

+ **Holes** that form naturally in stones are very auspicious and magical. If you look through the holes by the light of the moon, you should see visions and spirits.

- **Human body**–shaped stones bring good energy to the body parts being depicted and strengthen those areas.
- **Obelisks** are four-sided, pyramid-topped shapes and are wonderful energy activators, or manifesters. Write your wish down on paper and place it beneath an obelisk to bring that hope into reality.
- **Octahedrons,** eight-sided stones, bring order to chaos and are great for analysis and organization. They are also terrific for healing. Carry an octahedron crystal in your pocket if you are unwell, so you can feel better soon.
- **Pyramid**-shaped stones carry energy upward, toward their pointed tips. I have a beautiful little malachite pyramid that I keep on my computer simply because I love to look at it. When the need arises, however, I can place a dollar bill underneath it and visualize positive money energy flowing up out of the stone.
- **Rectangular** rocks and crystals represent the energy of God. In addition to symbolizing male energy and the phallus, this shape is symbolic of energy itself and electrical current. It also denotes protection. Rectangular stones are great for love and sex spells.
- **Round** stones represent the universe and the Goddess. They are symbols of spirituality, connection to the universe, femininity, and, of course, pregnancy. Round crystals can be used in all love spells to cause attraction.
- **Square** stones represent the earth and are harbingers of plenty and prosperity.
- **Triangular** stones are guardian stones and protect the wearers.

## Charm Boxes

Charm boxes, also known as spell boxes, are simple tools of magic you can easily make for yourself. Ancient cultures, particularly the Native Americans, Greeks, Celts, and Egyptians, used boxes for ceremonial magic and for the storage of sacred objects. Is not the famed biblical ark of the covenant a magical box? During medieval times, much spell work revolved around boxes. Even a young woman's hope chest is a type of magical box, filled with the wishes, intentions, and materials for a happy marriage.

Gem-magic boxes can either contain crystals of special importance to you or be adorned with gems you affix to the outside of the box. You can create a job-spell box with peridot or aventurine stones, green candles, patchouli incense, and dried ferns placed inside.

Make a love-spell box with two pieces of rose quartz, a pink candle, rose petals, and two copper pennies. Fashion a psychic-spell box using amethyst and quartz crystals, cloves, and rosemary.

## Mirrors of Mystery

Mirrors have been tools of magic since time immemorial. Shiny, smooth reflective surfaces have lent themselves so well to the imagination and intuition. It is little wonder that these portals to another world promote psychic awareness. Obsidian and other types of shimmering rocks and volcanic glasses presented themselves to primitive peoples as opportunities to communicate with unseen spirits, which is what we modern folk do when we are accessing energy.

When Harry Potter famously looked into his magic mirror, he awakened the masses to this tradition, and I have heard that sales of magic mirrors have skyrocketed. Throughout history, people looking for answers have used mirrors and even bowls filled with ink to peer into another dimension. Gazing balls and pools have also served for dealing with the divine.

You can make your own magic mirror and power it with crystals. First, get a round dime-store mirror, preferably with a plastic or wooden frame for ease of securely gluing appliqués. Make sure the frame has a lot of surface area on which to affix your gems. From any New Age store or rock shop, purchase fifty to 100 small crystals—various quartzes and semiprecious stones of a similar shape and small size. You can use a rainbow of colors unless you have a particular affinity for any certain stone. For example, amethyst is my birthstone, so I prefer to use an all-amethyst magic mirror. I simply feel more connected to this lovely, purple semiprecious gem.

Clean the frame with a soft, dry cloth and spread clear-drying glue onto it. One at a time, place the crystal pebbles into the glue in any pattern you desire. I have seen lovely versions of concentric circles of color following the spectrum, beginning with deepest, darkest red garnet stones inside and circling out to the palest purple pebbles and finally a layer of the clearest quartz. I have seen gorgeous pebble spirals and paisleys, and so many other patterns.

I know some gem magicians who have several magic mirrors for different kinds of questing and querying. A mirror of peridot, the birthstone of Leo, is good for looking at issues of self-image and matters centering around you. A ruby mirror (made of the highly affordable rough rubies) is perfect for matters relating to love, and a jade mirror will aid in money matters. Water signs (Cancer, Scorpio, and Pisces) would do well to make magic mirrors from sea glass and seashells they have gathered during walks on the beach. Anyone who feels drawn to the ocean will also benefit from a seashell magic mirror. Many of us go for walks on the beach or along water when we are searching for answers. A magic mirror of shells can be twice as effective at helping you find your answers!

Amethyst is still tops in my book, and I recommend a mirror adorned with this stone as a very dependable tool of magic. Amethyst is a good balancing stone and is also one of the most intuition-boosting of all gems.

## Swords and Knives

To make your own swords and knives, or *athames* (pronounced a-THAW-mays), you can affix crystals of your choice onto metalwork you purchase at a New Age store or from a sword specialist. Or, if you purchase an athame that already has crystals, you can charge your sword so it is imbued with your energy. The idea of the sword is that you wield it within the spirit world to keep bad energy and negativity at bay. With your sword in your hand, you are the master or mistress of your domain; you rule your circle of magic. The *bolline* is a usually white-handled knife that is used for making other tools; it can be used only within the magical circle, the boundary you form by marking the four corners and the four directions through speaking ritual.

## Cauldrons

Important tools used in magic rituals, cauldrons are typically iron kettles. You can make a symbolic cauldron, however, out of any concave or bowl-like object, such as a large stone or crystal geode.

## Magic Cord

This is a rope that binds magic to you and is ideally made from strands of red wool or ribbon. Nine feet long, it is braided and tied into a loop at one end to represent feminine energy and left loose or frayed at the opposing end to signify the complementary male energy. Crystal beads woven onto the strands of the rope can compound its magical quality. I recommend that you use clear quartz crystal beads, which are energy amplifiers, but you can use special stones for various effects: rose quartz for love, citrine for grounding, jade for prosperity and success in work, blue lapis for creativity, and amethyst for improved intuition and psychic ability. The descriptionary in Part Two of this book will guide you to other crystal bead options.

## *Magic Bottles*

In use since Elizabethan times, magic bottles, or spell bottles, can function as guardians. Called witch bottles in the 1600s in England, they were originally used to hold objects for magical uses. They have largely fallen out of use, but you can customize magic bottles for yourself with crystal stoppers for a variety of reasons. You can put one in your garden for healthy plants, on the mantel to protect your home, next to your bed for love and happiness, and in the kitchen for good health. These magic bottles are mostly used for protection, but you can also place into them symbols of your dreams and desires, such as a flower for peace, rosemary for remembrance, and cinnamon for the spice of life.

Magic bottles are very easy to make, as you can easily glue the crystals of your choice onto the lid or cork top or place them inside. Here are a few to try:

For luck with money, place three pennies and some pyrite or jade into a bottle and put it on your desk at home or your workplace. Shake the magic jar whenever you think about your finances, and your fortune will improve in three days.

For love, place a rosebud or rose petal, rose essential oil, and rose quartz into a bottle and keep it at your bedside. Each night, burn a pink candle anointed with the oil from your love-magic bottle. On the seventh day, your prospects for romance will brighten!

For a peaceful and secure home, take a teaspoon of soil from outside your house (or the closest park) and place it into a bottle with some smoky topaz or brown jasper. Place the bottle into the pot of a plant near the entrance of your home. Every time you water the plant, think about the sanctity of your home. As your plant grows, so will the tranquillity of your residence.

## Purification Broom

To purify your home, you need this special broom. A home purification is handy for clearing away bad energy after a squabble with your loved one, a bout of the blues, or just about any upset you need to get out of your personal space. I would go so far as to suggest that you sweep the negative energy outside every morning to freshen your surroundings and make room for the good energy that you want in your life. Bear in mind, this is not white glove—type cleaning; it is a symbolic act that is quite effective in maintaining your home as a personal sanctuary.

You can make your own purification broom from straw bound together and attached to a fallen tree branch, or you can add mojo to a store-bought broom. Wrap copper wire around your broom or use it to bind the straw to the stick, as Venus-ruled copper lends an aura of beauty and keeps negativity at bay. Attach crystals to the handle with glue to boost your broom. Recommended crystals for space clearing and purification are:

+ **amber** for cheeriness,
+ **blue lace agate** for tranquillity,
+ **coral** for well-being,
+ **jet** for absorption of bad energy,
+ **onyx** for protection,
+ **petrified wood** for security,
+ **tiger's-eye** for protecting your psyche from energy-draining powers, and
+ **turquoise** for relaxation and calmness.

## Tips 'n' Tricks

### PARKING PENDANT

Hang a red jasper crystal attached to a string on your rearview mirror in your car and your parking problems will soon be over. When you need a spot, touch the jasper and say, "Squat, Squat, find me a spot!" Remember to always give thanks to the parking gods and goddesses to remain in their favor.

### Scrying Mirrors and Crystal Balls

Scrying is the art of divining by looking into an appropriate surface. It could be water, a mirror on the wall, a crystal ball, or a slab of rock. For that matter, some people are quite talented at seeing visions in the flames of fire or in the bottom of a teacup. Smooth, neutral surfaces are much better and less distracting, however.

I like to think that a chunk of shiny black obsidian was the first scrying mirror. We know the ancients had special prophets and priestesses who engaged in foretelling the future, and they were making and using tools of their trade from various crystals at hand. No doubt they would be delighted to know we are still using crystal balls made from translucent quartz and mysterious volcanic obsidian! I cleanse mine before and after each use with rainwater that has sat through at least one day of sun and one night of moonlight, but rituals can get as elaborate as you want!

Scrying has been used since biblical times and is even mentioned in Genesis chapter 44, verses 4–5 (NKJV). Queen Elizabeth I entrusted all matters of the heavens and the unseen to John Dee, a brilliant mathematician and metaphysician. He used a mirror of polished black obsidian, and his legacy led succeeding magicians and psychics to prefer black mirrors. Dee employed scrying to great effect in calling upon certain angels. He reported hearing knocking and even voices that sounded like an owl screeching during sessions.

Scrying is the mantic art of gazing onto a surface and receiving information in the form of visions. It is said that this gives us a more direct connection to the *Akashic record,* the theory of cosmic memory storage espoused by the theosophist Rudolf Steiner.

Scrying can be used for myriad purposes in addition to divining the past, present, and future. You can contact spirit guides, improve your skills of creative visualization, and even use it as a gateway to the astral plane. As with crystal balls and other sacred tools, you should polish mirrors with a clean cotton cloth and store them in a special protective bag.

Quartz crystal balls have an inherent power that you have to practice working with. They have been part of our folklore, myth, magic, and metaphysics for a long time. The great philosopher and physician Paracelsus made the claim during the height of the Renaissance that what he called conjuring crystals needed to be used in "observing everything rightly, earning and understanding what was." I love that they are in fairy tales and Disney stories, too. That shows how ingrained crystal balls are in our culture and collective mind-set. Even people who avoid anything too witchy know of the power of crystal balls!

Crystal balls have their own authority and wield a large influence on the development of our psychic abilities. When you gaze into a crystal ball, it is possible to see into the fabric of time, both the past and the future. What you see could be a delineated vision or a flickering, wispy suggestion of images. You have to practice and hone your attunement with the energy of the crystal ball. Many psychics use crystal balls in their readings, and some report seeing images of clients' auras in the ball. What you have to get really clear on is how you interpret what you see. Gleaning information about people's lives is a huge responsibility, and you need to feel sure about what you are reading. One way is to learn to trust your center of intuition in your body. For me (and for many other people) it is a gut feeling —literally in my stomach. I have a feeling of surety, of knowing, and I speak from that. If I don't get any such bodily sensation, I simply explain that I don't know what I'm reading or I'm not really "getting anything." It is far better to say you don't know than to fake it.

You can sharpen your psychic skills by working with a partner. Sit directly across from your partner with a crystal ball between you. Close your eyes halfway and look *at* the ball and *into* the ball while harnessing your entire mind. Empty out all other thoughts and focus as hard as you can. Your third eye should begin to open, and the vision and intuition will come from there and project into the crystal ball. As you train your mind, the patterns will become clearer and your impressions will become surer. You should trust that what you are seeing is real and find a place of knowing, as I do with my stomach. Express to your partner what you are seeing. Then listen to your partner as she reveals her visions to you. After at least three rounds of individual reading and revealing, share visions at the same time and learn whether you are seeing the same things!

A mental practice to try on your own is this crystal-ball meditation: In a darkened room, sit holding your crystal ball in the palms of both of your hands. Touch it to your heart and then gently touch it to your forehead where the third eye resides. Then hold the ball in front of your eyes and, sitting very still, gaze into it for at least three minutes. Envision pure white light in the ball and hold that image. Practice the white-light visualization for up to a half hour and then rest your mind, your eyes, and your crystal ball. If you do this every day, within a month you will start to become adept at crystal-ball gazing.

## Tips 'n' Tricks

### WHY SCRY?

If you have ever experienced a problem in your life that no one else could help you with, a scrying mirror or crystal can offer counsel. Any time you feel the need for insight and answers, scrying can lend illumination. Are you stymied at work? Are you restless and don't know why? Do you suspect someone isn't being honest with you? Try scrying! Here are scrying crystals to use for intuition power:

- **Amethyst** opens your own psychic abilities.
- **Azurite with malachite** can help with studying and brainstorming ideas.
- **Bloodstone** guards you against anyone trying to deceive you.
- **Celestite** gives you the very special help of angel-powered insight and advice.
- **Chrysocolla** helps you to see and resolve relationship difficulties.
- **Lapis lazuli** leads the way if you are looking for a new job.
- **Selenite** can be used under moonlight for pleasant visions of your future.

Choosing a crystal ball should not be undertaken lightly; this is a deeply personal tool that has its own energy and will also become imbued with your energy. Think of it as a container for a great deal of your energy and make sure it feels right for you. It should have the right heft in your hand and feel comfortable for you and you alone. Do not allow anyone else to touch your crystal ball. If by chance it happens, simply place it in a bowl of sea salt overnight and it will be cleansed of outside energy and influence.

Highly polished and glasslike spheres of beryl and quartz crystal have been in use for many thousands of years. Healers, shamans, witch doctors, and medicine men have been using the bones of the earth for divination since time immemorial. The Celtic folks and Druids favored beryl as their scrying crystal of choice. Beryl still has a well-earned reputation as the stone of power. The Middle Ages and the Renaissance saw a far-flung use of crystal for seeing the future. The mythical wizard Merlin, of Arthurian legend, kept his crystal ball with him at all times! Pure quartz crystal balls are quite pricey but are worth the expense if you are serious about harnessing your intuition and using it for the good. Most people I know who use crystal balls, including many healers and teachers, see cloudy and smoky images, so do not expect your experience to be like going to the movies! Each and every crystal ball is unique and has its own energy. Here are a few examples:

+ **Amethyst** offers advice on business matters and is especially good for lawyers and writers.

+ **Beryl** helps you find anything you have lost—keys, jewelry, money, people!

+ **Obsidian** is the karma stone and helps you see and resolve past-life issues.

+ **Quartz crystal** can put you in touch with helpful spirit guides who foretell events.

+ **Selenite** is particularly useful with any matters regarding hearth and home.

+ **Smoky quartz** connects you with nature spirits and shows you what to avoid in your life.

## Cleaning Your Crystal Ball

After the first thirty-three days of tuning in with your new crystal ball, you should give it a good cleaning, both physically and energetically. Thirty-three is a power number and is exactly the right amount of time to wait so that your crystal ball is permeated with your personal psychic energy. I recommend keeping it with you—in a pocket or, if it is smaller, even in a little pouch around your neck. The constant interaction with your body will get you and your crystal ball in sync.

To thoroughly cleanse the crystal, put in a bowl of sea salt for seven days. Treat your crystal ball as the precious thing it is. Keep it in a soft cloth; I prefer a dark blue silk bag. Never store your crystal ball in a synthetic material—it came from the earth and needs to stay connected to the earth's grounding energy. If you are like me and have slightly sticky, well-lotioned hands, you simply need to wash the crystal in warm water after each use and then wipe it with a soft, natural-fabric cloth; all will be well. Regard your crystal ball with the highest respect, the highest regard, and the highest mind, and it will give you a lifetime of great service. Also, remain mindful that you are using it for the purposes of universal love and healing and these effects shall be so.

*Chapter Five*

# CRYSTAL
# CONJURING
# AND
# STONE SPELLS

**M**agic resides inside of us; we create it with our thoughts and actions. It is our deepest personal power, and we are all born with it. This is the energy we draw from each and every day. The goal of magic, including gem magic, is to bring about needed change. It is how we make things better for ourselves, for the people in our lives, and for our world. From an inner place of intention, we are working to bring about change for peace, prosperity, love, health, home, spirituality, and other areas in our lives that are always in need of improvement. The stone spells and crystal conjurations on the following pages are "recipes" you can begin to use to create happiness right now.

## UNLEASHING YOUR PERSONAL POWER

To begin using your magical powers, you must first set the stage, the perfect environment in which to incubate your ideas. You'll do this by building a stone shrine, your touchstone for daily conjuring and contemplation. By preparing your home and sparking your inner flame, you can clear away personal blocks and invite in the friendly spirits who will aid and abet your supernatural pursuits. It is of the utmost importance to have in your home a shrine or an altar, a power center, where you can keep your stones and perform rituals and spells. This is your energy source where you can renew yourself and your spirits every day. The more you use your altar, the more it will build up energy, and the more effective your spells will be.

On a low table, place a white scarf and candles from each of the colors of the spectrum: white, violet, blue, green, yellow, orange, pink, red, and black. Place them in the miraculous arching shape of a rainbow. Take amber incense and place it in a quartz crystal bowl at the center of the rainbow. Amber is good for creativity and healing and also contains crystalline grains of rock resin from Mother Nature. Keep a wand of sage or a smudging stick in a fireproof bowl or seashell on your altar and use it to clear the energy and sanctify the space every day.

Next, place symbols on the altar that reflect your personal power and spiritual aspirations. I keep fresh wildflowers in a vase beside a statue of a goddess pouring water of wisdom, symbolizing Aquarius. I also have abalone shells, which represent my Piscean nature, aligned with a magnetite obelisk and a rock-crystal ball. Let your imagination run wild! Use religious icons and images or photos that have special meaning—whatever expresses your innermost spirit. If you have an obelisk or pyramid on your altar, you can use it for manifestation by placing your desires and wishes on paper beneath the crystal.

Keep the basic principles of feng shui in mind and put prosperity stones in your far-left money corner, and romance rocks in your far-right love corner.

The crystals you select should be a completely personal choice. Browse your favorite lapidary or New Age shop and see what you are drawn to and resonate most with. Here are some crystals you can choose for specific spell work and energy you want in your life and environment:

  + **for creativity**: amazonite, aventurine, carnelian, chrysolite, chrysoprase, citrine, green tourmaline, malachite, yellow fluorite;

  + **for intuition**: amethyst, azurite, celestite, lapis lazuli, moonstone, selenite, smoky quartz, sodalite, star sapphire, yellow calcite;

- **for love:** amethyst, aventurine, magnetite, rhodochrosite, rose quartz, twinned rock crystal;
- **for prosperity:** bloodstone, carnelian, citrine, dendritic agate, diamond, garnet, hawk's-eye, moss agate, peridot, ruby, tiger's-eye, topaz, yellow sapphire;
- **for protection:** amber, Apache tear, chalcedony, citrine, green calcite, jade, jet, smoky quartz;
- **for self-assurance:** azurite, chalcedony, chrysocolla, green tourmaline, hematite, rutilated quartz, tiger's-eye;
- **for serenity:** amber, aventurine, blue jade, dioptase, Herkimer diamond, jasper, kunzite, moonstone, onyx, peridot, quartz, rhodonite;
- **for success:** carnelian, obsidian, quartz, selenite, sodalite, topaz;
- **for vigor:** agate, aventurine, bloodstone, calcite, chalcedony, citrine, dioptase, emerald, garnet, orange calcite, ruby, topaz;
- **for wisdom:** emerald, fluorite, Herkimer diamond, moldavite, serpentine, yellow calcite.

## PHASES OF THE MOON

Performing a spell at the optimal time in the lunar cycle will maximize your power. As you read the rites and rituals in this book, keep this elemental magic in mind: Each lunar cycle begins with a *new* phase, when the Moon lies between the Sun and Earth so that the illuminated side cannot be seen from Earth. The Moon gradually waxes until it has moved to the opposite side of Earth. When it has reached the far side of Earth, its lit side faces us in the *full-moon* phase. It then wanes until it reaches the new-moon phase again.

The entire cycle takes a month, during which the Moon orbits Earth. To determine the pattern of astrological signs governing the Moon, you will need a celestial guide or almanac. My favorite is Llewellyn's *Daily Planetary Guide*. The Moon moves from sign to sign every two or three days.

# MAKING MAGIC

### Astral Azurite Spell

The great psychic and healer Edgar Cayce used this blue beauty for achieving the remarkable meditative states during which he had astoundingly accurate visions and prophetic dreams. Indeed, azurite helps achieve a high state of mental clarity and powers of concentration. If you can't find the answer to a problem in the here and now, try looking for solutions on the astral plane. Write the problem down on paper and place it under a small azurite overnight on a windowsill so it collects moonlight.

At 11:11 a.m., lie comfortably in a quiet and darkened room with the azurite stone placed over your third eye on your forehead. Clear your mind of everything for eleven minutes and meditate. Sit up and listen for the first thing that comes into your mind—it should be the answer or a message regarding the issue at hand. Write down the words you receive. The rest of the day you will be in a state of grace and higher mind during which you will hear information and answers to help guide you in many aspects of your life. If you, like me, enjoy this meditation, you may want to do it every day at 11:11 a.m. and every night at 11:11 p.m. I strongly suggest that you keep a journal of these "azurite answers." You may receive information that you won't understand until many years have passed, making the journal an invaluable resource and key to your very special life.

## Rocket-in-Your-Pocket Incantation

If you are like me, you can't exactly afford to buy a ruby on the spot. I have been gladdened lately by the appearance of $3-each rough rubies at the Psychic Eye Bookstore, a chain of metaphysical superstores. If one isn't near you, you can shop online at www.pebooks.com. Now those rubies I *can* buy on impulse!

Rubies are stones of great passion. Here is a simple way to light a fire by day that will ignite with your lover by night. Hold your ruby in your left hand over your heart and speak aloud three times:

> *"I can feel the heat*
> *Of your skin*
> *And your mouth;*
> *I can taste the kisses sweet.*
> *Your hands on me,*
> *My hands on you;*
> *Oh, lover, hear my song.*
> *Tonight, we will be as one*
> *All night long."*

Now carry your heart-warmed red ruby in your pocket all day long. Don't forget to give your lover a call and invite him or her over for a long and lovely night.

## Ecstatic Elixir

An elixir is a very simple potion made by placing a crystal or gemstone in a glass of water for at least seven hours. Then you remove the stone and drink the water, which now carries the vibrational energy of the stone, the very essence of the crystal. This is one of the easiest ways to receive crystal healing and is immediate.

The red stones always hold a lust for life. So, for the Ecstatic Elixir, we are going to push the envelope here and put as many red stones into our potion as we can! Place the following into a glass of water: carnelian, garnet, rough ruby, red coral, red jade, jasper, red sardonyx, cuprite, aventurine, and red calcite. If you don't have all of these, just mix and match. Even a single rough ruby and a tiny chunk of jasper is a lot of love in a jar!

Place the Ecstatic Elixir on the love corner of your room or altar. Light amber incense and a red candle and speak this spell: "This jade is my joy, the garnet my grace."

Leave the water on your altar for seven hours or overnight, and drink it upon awakening. Your life energy will quicken, and you should feel very upbeat and good to go.

## Presentation Pendulum

If you are a creative person getting ready to present your work to the world, you can wear a talisman of your own making to ensure a positive outcome. Many performers, artists, musicians, and other inspired folks have lucky pieces of clothing or some other token that gives them courage to put themselves forth in the best possible manner.

Gem magic is perfect for creating your own success in this sort of endeavor. Put a talismanic power stone in your pocket or purse and you will have an aura of achievement all around you. When choosing your talisman, keep these pointers in mind:

**Red stones,** such as garnet, ruby, carnelian, red jasper, and jade, are excellent for attracting positive attention, such as publicity for your recital or poetry reading. For a speech, a performance, a presentation, or a show of your art, wear red jewelry.

**Green stones,** such as emerald and peridot, are wonderful for realizing your potential for wealth and successful new projects. If you are preparing for a possibly lucrative deal of your creative output—pitching a book or an art opening —you must wear green jewelry.

**Blue stones,** such as turquoise, topaz, lapis lazuli, and sapphire, help you to see clearly and without obstruction. If you are trying to empower someone to see and share your creative vision, blue gems are right for you.

### Charm-Bracelet Charm

Most people don't realize that the classic charm bracelet is decorated with magical symbols representing the wearer's wishes. For wealth, wear a Roman coin on your bracelet. For love, try a heart.

### Pinkie Power

For protection, a pure silver ring worn on the right pinkie has the greatest magical power, especially when engraved with your birth sign, or astrological glyph, and the sacred pentagram. To instill the ring with protective power, clasp it over your heart and call out: "Ring of Silver, shield and encircle me. Blessed be."

### Calling All Angels

You can access your intuition and prophetic capabilities and also call for angelic assistance with this Wednesday ritual. You'll need these ingredients: one celestite stone and one palmful each of ground cloves, dried sage, and amber resin.

With a mortar and pestle, mix the herbs together. Place the heavenly blue celestite in front of you and say aloud three times:

> *"Calling all angels!*
> *Come and play.*

> *Be with me now*
> *And show me how*
> *To make my way."*

Burn the herbs in your fireplace or in a dish while looking at the celestite and concentrating on a question, such as whether to take a new job or end a relationship. Use this time to cleanse your mind of all concerns, worries, and thoughts, making way for pure insight. Answers will come, and angels *always* give you a sign that they have visited. It can come in the form of an amazing coincidence, a song on the radio, or some other sweet surprise.

## Color Craft

Candle magic is a mainstay of gem magic. I burn candles every night and take them with me when I am traveling. For this exercise to work, simply apply the basic precepts of color magic: Have a clear intention of your desired outcome and choose the appropriate color candle from the following list. On the corresponding day, begin burning the candle on your altar or any special place in your home. Repeat this ritual for seven consecutive days with the same color candle.

+ **Sunday:** The Sun rules this day; use gold or red to affect a boss, a promotion, health, fame, or success.
+ **Monday:** The Moon rules this day; use silver or orange to affect the home, subordinates, or emotions.
+ **Tuesday:** Mars rules; use yellow to affect aggressions, sex, conflict, or confidence.
+ **Wednesday:** Mercury rules; use green to affect communication, study, or intelligence.

- ✦ **Thursday**: Jupiter rules; use blue to affect medical and legal issues, money, spirit, integrity, safety, or security.
- ✦ **Friday**: Venus rules; use indigo to affect aesthetics and beauty, marriage, relationships, theater, art, music, or family.
- ✦ **Saturday**: Saturn rules; use black to affect judgment, obstacles, or property.

## *Employment Incantation*

Here is one of the ways I got a great job on my first day in San Francisco: Light a gold candle and place it in a special place beside a crystal of pyrite, otherwise known as fool's gold. Repeat this incantation eight times while holding the gold in your right hand and holding a vision of yourself at the desired job:

> *"I see the perfect job for me;*
> *I see a place of plenty.*
> *Upon my heart's desire I am set;*
> *My new boss will never regret.*
> *This job will come to me NOW;*
> *Harm to none, I vow. So mote it be."*

## *Revenue Stream*

After your Employment Incantation, you might want to immerse yourself in the waters of prosperity with a money bath. This particular ritual is most effective if practiced on Thursday night during a new or full moon. Pour apple green or lemon verbena essential oil into running bathwater and bathe by the light of a single green candle. As you close your eyes, meditate on your truest desires. What does personal prosperity mean to you? What do you really need and what do you really want? When you are clear about your answers, put on *all* of your green gem jewelry—peridot, green jade, tourmaline, malachite, and so on. Focus on the candle flame while whispering:

> *"Here and now, my intention is set.*
> *New luck will be mine and all needs will be met.*
> *With harm to none and plenty for all. Blessed be."*

## Burning Away Bad Luck

The world can overwhelm us at times with problems relating to work, finances, and all manner of problems that get in the way and want to stay. But these problems are *not* beyond your control! The ultimate time to release bad luck is immediately after a full moon or any Friday the thirteenth.

If you have been on an unlucky streak, get yourself a big black candle, an obsidian sphere (or at least an obsidian crystal), a piece of white paper, a black ink pen, a cancellation stamp (readily available at any stationery store), and a big flat rock that is slightly concave in the center. Write on the paper what you wish to be freed from; this is your release request. Place the candle and the obsidian on the flat rock and light the candle near an open window so the negative energy will leave your home. While the candle burns, intone:

> *"Waxing moon, most wise Cybele,*
> *From me this burden please dispel.*
> *Upon this night so clear and bright*
> *I release ___ to the moon tonight."*

Bury the candle in your garden for thirteen minutes. Take your stamp and mark the paper "cancelled." Put the candle out, fold the paper away from you, and place it under the flat stone. Repeat this process for twelve more nights (thirteen total). On the last night, which should ideally be the beginning of the new-moon phase, burn the paper and bury the candle, paper ashes, and flat rock far from your home. Give thanks to the moon for assisting you, and LET GO of bad luck!

### Lucky-Stone Spell

Another charm for solvency is to take seven tiny turquoise stones and put them on your windowsill during a full moon for seven hours. Then pick up the stones, and while holding them in the palm of your hand, speak this wish-spell:

> *"Luck be quick, luck be kind.*
> *And by lucky seven, good luck will be mine."*

Carry these lucky stones with you in a bright blue bag and be on the lookout for blessings to shower down upon you. You might receive a gift, win free services, or literally find money in your path.

### Money Bags

Rather than chasing money or possessions, you can simply draw them to you with wisdom from days gone by. A tiny green pouch filled with the herb vervain, a silver dollar, and lapis lazuli or peridot, is a powerful tool for making positive change in your life and attracting good fortune.

Prepare your attraction pouch during a waxing moon (ideally when the Moon is in the sign of Taurus). Hold the pouch over frankincense incense and let the smoke bless the bag as you speak:

> *"The moon is a silver coin;*
> *I carry lunar abundance with me.*
> *Blessings upon thee and me."*

## Abalone Abundance

Thursdays are named for Jupiter, or Jove, originally Thor of Norse mythology, who represents joviality, expansion, and all things abundant. Here is a Jupiterian Thursday spell that will bring excellent opportunities your way.

On a Thursday, go for a walk in the woods, in the park, or on the beach. Bring an abalone seashell and two votive candles—one green and one purple. Gather wildflowers, preferably yellow ones, such as dandelions. Place the candles inside the abalone shell. Encircle the shell with the flowers and any gifts from nature that appeal to you—iridescent feathers, smooth driftwood, sandblasted sea glass. Stand in front of your natural altar and consider the wonderful, full life you are going to enjoy. Light the candles and say:

> *"As above, so below,*
> *The wisdom of the world shall freely flow.*
> *To perfect possibility, I surrender. So mote it be."*

## Almond Attraction

Using almonds and almond oil is a simple way to attract into your life whatever you want more of—love, money, a new home, you decide! The great psychic Edgar Cayce even believed that eating five almonds a day could prevent cancer. I anoint myself with almond oil every morning as a kind of self-blessing for health and wealth. A little dab of this attraction oil will go far for you, too.

If you are feeling a financial pinch, try rubbing some almond oil on your wallet and visualize it filling up with bills. Rubbing this essence on magnetite can miraculously bring your wishes directly to you. A drop or two on green candles will also make an appreciable difference.

Almond oil works quickly because it is ruled by Mercury, the god of speed and communication, who operates in the realm of the air.

### Lovely Lodestones

Stones, crystals, and gems are regarded as the purest forms of the earth's abundance. Whenever you get a new piece of jewelry with a stone or gem or decorate your home or garden with rocks and pebbles, show gratitude for these gifts from nature. Sprinkle thyme, daisy blossoms, and ground cinnamon on your garden path and on your doorstep. Also, burn this mix in your incense holder and chant:

> *"Mother Nature, I thank you for the strength*
> *and bounty of your stones and bones.*
> *Your beauty is reflected now and forever. Blessed be."*

Your gratitude will be rewarded tenfold, and you will enjoy a shower of crystals and gems in your life from Mother Nature, who enjoys getting credit for her good works!

### Thrice-Blessed Crystals

You can perform a blessing on a single stone and keep it with you at all times. I keep an amethyst crystal chunk on my bed stand and another one that is a candleholder in my office. As a Pisces, I want my birthstone energy with me for strength, stability, and a love connection with the universe.

Choose a crystal to become your touchstone. Begin charging your crystal on your altar during a full moon. Light a white candle for purification and then place your hands on the stone. Chant thrice:

> *"Goddess of Night, moon of this night,*
> *Fill my stone with your white light.*
> *Instill this stone with your magic and might;*
> *Surround it with your loving sight.*
> *So mote it be."*

## MOONSTONE MIRROR

Moonstone is a psychic mirror, especially for females. Wise women of ancient India were the first to figure this out. If you are feeling out-of-sorts or off-center, turn to this lovely stone, sacred to the shining orb in our night sky. Under moonlight, gaze first at the moon and then at your smooth, round moonstone and look for the answer to your personal mystery. A message will come to you in the form of a dream this night.

---

Perform this spell three nights in a row. Then you can begin to draw energy from it. Your sanctified stone will be a source of strength, wisdom, and love you can turn to whenever you are down and in need of a boost. And, best of all, you can take it with you!

### Ambition Amulet

Fill a little pouch of muslin or cotton with pieces of tiger's-eye, cedar, and carnelian. Carry it in your pocket or purse to give you that extra little push of motivation to jump over any hurdles or difficult tasks at work.

### Candled Crystals

I made candles as a young girl, and that hobby has now grown into a full-blown obsession. A few years ago, it occurred to me that I could have "stained-glass" candles by mixing big crystal chunks into the wax inside the mold. An even easier way to do this is to take a soft beeswax pillar candle and stud the sides and top with crystal pieces that cost just pennies per pound. I save mine from the melted candles and reuse them again and again.

## Stained-Glass Spell

Recently, I have been wishing and hoping for peace in this world of ours, as have most of us. I have been making, burning, and giving away candles with the word "peace" written with crystals embedded in the soft candle wax.

If possible, perform this spell during a full-moon night for the greatest effect. Place your stained-glass peace candle on your altar and light rose incense, which represents love and unity. Light the candle and chant:

*"I light this candle for hope,*
*I light this candle for love,*
*I light this candle for unity,*
*I light this candle for the good of all the world*
*That we should live in peace. And so it shall be."*

Sit in front of your altar and meditate, eyes closed, for a few minutes while visualizing peace in the world. Let the candle burn completely for full charging.

## Crystal Feng Shui for Love and Happiness

Place these objects in your home to attract loving energy—new friends and relationships:

+ two crystals of rose quartz of equivalent size,
+ pink, orange, or red fabric,
+ two red candles, and
+ images of two butterflies.

## Candle Conjuration for a Happy Home

Choose a brown crystal, such as jasper, smoky quartz, selenite, or brown jade, to improve and secure positive, grounding energy in your home. Anoint two candles with rose oil and light some cinnamon incense. Place your brown crystal in front of the candles. Meditate to clear your mind of any distractions, which is essential to opening the mental and spiritual space necessary to create. Once you feel focused, light a single leaf or sage bundle and say aloud:

> *"By my hand*
> *And by the blessing of the spirit,*
> *The fire of home and heart burns bright,*
> *Burns long,*
> *Burns eternal.*
> *I offer my home to*
> *New friends and new love.*
> *Welcome!"*

## Full-Moon Stone Invocation

The full moon is the most powerful time of the month and the perfect time to celebrate with special people in your life. The ritual will heighten your spirituality, your friendships, and your connection to the powers of the universe.

As I write this, it is a full moon in Libra, and I look forward to getting together with some of the sisterhood, some fellow Wicca chicks, and kicking up our heels in celebration of life and asking for what we need from the universe. We will wait until midnight, the traditional witching hour. We will gather in one of our favorite spots near water under the spring moonlight.

Here is our recipe for ritual: We place a large crystal—usually a geode, an amethyst chunk, or a big quartz or rock crystal—in the middle of the altar. We place a goblet of wine before an image of the Goddess. We all bring candles in sturdy, tempered-glass votives to light our way, and we perform a rite we learned from our elders. Each of us holds a crystal that is our touchstone.

You can perform this ritual in your home or garden or a sacred place of your choosing. Designate a leader who will perform all the incantations as the group forms a circle. Begin with the appointee chanting:

> *"Oh, lady of silver magic, we honor you here,*
> *In this place, sacred and safe.*
> *This circle is in your honor."*

The person in the northern point of the circle places her candle and her crystal on the ground as the leader chants:

> *"Blessed one, all earth is yours.*
> *May we all heal,*
> *May we all draw strength,*
> *May we grow."*

The person in the eastern point places her candle and her crystal on the ground while the leader chants:

> *"Oh, lady of laughter and joy, so is the sky yours, too.*
> *May the air be clear and pure,*
> *And the clouds sweet with wind and rain."*

The person at the southern point lays down her crystal and candle while the chanter speaks:

> *"Oh, lady of summer, each season is yours.*
> *May each spring bring flowers and crops for all."*

The person at the western point lays down her candle and crystal while the chanter speaks:

> *"Goddess of the waters,*
> *The rivers and the ocean are yours.*

> *May they once more flow crystal clear.*
> *Lady, we have built this circle in your honor.*
> *Be with us here now."*

Now each member of the circle goes to the altar and kneels, placing her candle and crystal on the altar. Each takes a sip from the goblet of wine and says:

> *"I toast thee, bright lady,*
> *In your honor. Blessed be."*

Then, they all pick up rattles and drums and sing and dance under the sparkling crystals in the sky.

### New-Moon Lover's Spell

On the next new-moon night, take the two pieces of rose quartz and place them on the floor in the center of your bedroom. Light two red candles and use this affirming chant:

> *"Beautiful crystal I hold this night,*
> *Flame with love for my delight.*
> *Goddess of Love, I ask of you,*
> *Guide me in the path that is true.*
> *Harm to none as love comes to me—*
> *This I ask and so it shall be!"*

### Inviting and Welcoming Benevolent Spirits

By now, you should have gathered up a collection of crystals that includes small rocks. Make a wind chime with them to use when you want to gather up the good energy of those unseen who can help protect you and drive away the not so helpful energy. Take a stick (a small piece of sea-smoothed driftwood is perfect);

tie string around chunks of any or all of these crystals that help you make contact with your guardian angels—celestite, aquamarine, muscovite, morganite, and selenite; and tie each string to the wood. Hang it in your home or wherever you want to make contact with the spirit world.

Welcome the spirits by blessing the new chime by smudging it with sage smoke. Jingle the chimes energetically while you speak this spell:

> *"I call upon my angels to guide joy to my door*
> *Such gladness as I receive, so I shall give*
> *By the moon and the stars*
> *I call upon my guardians*
> *To show me the best way to live.*
> *For this, I am grateful. Blessed be."*

# EXPERIMENTING ON YOUR OWN

There are so many kinds of rituals, from everyday actions to special incantations for high holy days such as Beltane (May Day) and Samhain (All Hallows Eve). You have sampled just a few spells and rituals here and have learned how you can wield gem magic in your life. After you have been practicing these crystal conjurations for a while, you can experiment with new variations, and they will most likely come naturally to you. Try the stones you are attracted to for your altar, and if you feel an affinity for a certain crystal, explore it in the resource section of this book and then discover for yourself how you can use that stone to suit your needs. Just think about the positive change you want in your life and create your personal spell book.

*Chapter Six*

# CRYSTAL HEALING
# AND
# CRYSTAL
# CONSCIOUSNESS

It is becoming widely known that crystals can be curative for the emotional body, the spiritual body, and the physical body. And, we have learned that crystals can interact electromagnetically with people. The prehistoric medicine men and shamans knew instinctively how to harness this stone power and use it to enhance or stimulate energy; they never doubted the power of the unseen. Modern shamans talk about the body in a different way; they are in tune with and are working with the *etheric body,* the subtle life force that sustains the physical body and serves as the matrix for the metabolic functions. They work with the system of *chakras* (points of energy in the astral body that are associated with various parts of the physical body) and endeavor to make sure everything is in proper alignment. Illness beginning with misalignment of either the etheric body or physical body can result in a domino effect of maladies. Imbalance in the etheric body can cause low energy; depression; stress-related diseases such as shingles, ulcers, and migraines; and any number of other serious physical issues.

It is important to recognize that crystals work in a subtle manner and are useful for dealing with causes. Crystal medicine isn't going to cure ulcers or migraines, but it can get at the root of the problems and is marvelous when used in connection with Western medicine. I am thrilled that my hospital here in the San Francisco Bay Area—California Pacific Medical Center, on Webster Street in San Francisco's Pacific Heights—has an Institute for Health & Healing. This integrative medicine center has a Healing Store that sells crystals, healing stones and herbs, finger labyrinths, and aromatherapy and meditation aids and offers classes in Eastern approaches to healing, such as yoga and tai chi. We are living in wonderful times when you see medical doctors also practicing alternative and integrative healing methodologies.

# CRYSTAL CLARITY

Crystal healing requires consciousness on the part of the end user. So, you must be aware of the potential of a given stone and wear it mindfully. Following is a veritable encyclopedia of crystals and the special qualities they avail to anyone with crystal consciousness. I have also noticed in myself and in fellow gem fans that certain affinities between people and crystals will make themselves known and should be paid attention to. If you are attracted to a certain stone, by all means, investigate. Learn what that gem or crystal is about and examine your present state to see if you are in need of its particular properties. I went through a two-year period of being very attracted to quartz striated with little streaks of gold. Gold can very much intensify the healing power of the quartz, cleansing the aura and awakening all the chakras. I found out later that I had cancer, which, thankfully, is in the past—recent past, but nevertheless, my doctors tell me I am "clean." Unbeknownst to me, I was gravitating toward a stone that offered just that—cleansing.

My friend Nancy and I love to shop together. On the weekends we browse through bookshops, take in a movie and lunch, and then go to our favorite little shop, Planet Weavers, a sort of metaphysical five-and-dime. I noticed there was a time when Nancy kept buying citrine, a yellow or gold form of quartz. Nancy is much less New Age than I; her feet are firmly planted on the ground.

But I was aware that she was going through a really hard time at work with a very critical supervisor. She always seemed to be getting into trouble and never saw that she might have been at fault in some way. After she wore her favorite citrine-chip necklace, her path at work got smoother, and she and her boss started getting along. Citrine can aid in being able to receive and hear criticism gainfully. It certainly worked for her. So, please *do* listen to sudden stone attractions. Your body or subconscious may be sending you a very important message!

## DARNING YOUR AURA

We have all encountered psychic vampires, whether we know it or not. The problem is, your aura will know it because psychic vampires tear away little pieces of your *chi,* or life force, leaving holes in your aura. You can identify the places that need patching because they will become noticeably cold as you pass a crystal over them. Pick your favorite stone from amethyst, citrine, or any quartz and run it all around you at a distance of about 3 inches. Make note of the cold spots and lay the crystal on those places for up to five minutes, until the spot feels warmer. You will have repaired the holes in your etheric body and should begin to feel a pleasant sense of renewed wholeness once again.

Here's another technique: crystal combing. It sounds odd, but you will become an aficionado immediately after you have felt the wonderfully soothing results. The beautiful pink kunzite is amazing as a mental-management crystal. Take the crystal and brush it in gentle, slow, downward strokes from the top of your head, the crown chakra, to the bottom of your feet. The next time you feel overwhelmed by anxiety, try this and you will feel more relaxed and in control afterward.

Kunzite is also a heart mender, touching upon the heart chakra to bring inner peace, clear away old romantic wounds, and get rid of emotional baggage.

You can place a chunk of kunzite upon your chest, meditate with it, and feel the healing energy flow in.

## CRANIUM-CALMING CRYSTALS

Lapis lazuli has been used to treat headaches for millennia. My dear friend Nancy suffers from migraines and cluster headaches. I gave Nancy some earrings with lovely blue lapis settings to help her with this chronic condition, and she has reported great success. These headaches can have many causes and triggers; my beloved amber essence oil was one until we figured that out! The main causes are stress, anxiety, and various food triggers. Oddly enough, amber in crystal form alleviated Nancy's heinous headaches, seemingly absorbing the negative energy. Amethyst and turquoise are also good for this. Several stones are good for stomach illness; citrine and moonstone create calm, in this case, that stops the stomach unrest from signaling the brain to have a headache.

## PAIN-RELIEF PRISMS

When you feel pain somewhere in your body, it is a small voice that needs to be listened to. It could be old energy that needs to be released or a blockage or imbalance. I was in a hit-and-run auto accident where I was hit by a drunk driver who plowed through a red light and totaled my car, and very nearly me. As I hit the brake, my foot and ankle were shattered, rather like a porcelain teacup thrown with great force. The doctors wanted to amputate my leg, but I managed to talk them out of it. I had to learn to walk again, but I can walk and even dance and run again after lots of physical therapy and healing. But nowadays whenever I hit the brake too hard, I feel pain because my body remembers. The tissue and bones hold the memory imprint of that awful day and the terrible trauma.

Crystals have very mild and serene ways of tranquilizing negative energy and releasing the pain. In my case, I ever so gently rub the crystal across my ankle. (Carnelian works well because it is said to be good for healing bones, but quartz can also serve the purpose.) The stone feels cool and calming as the pain dissipates. I also visualize the pain going into the crystal, and the crystal forming a prism that contains the pain. At first, this was very frightening for me, but I found that rose quartz helped me deal with my fear. I placed the rose quartz over the heart area, the solar plexus, and as the crystal touched upon the heart chakra, I felt the fear dissolving while the pain gradually lessened. Turquoise and carnelian are also good for this.

I once had a copper bracelet set with onyx, coral, and turquoise from a Cherokee reservation that was so effective at treating wrist pain that it finally disintegrated from overuse. Copper is unmatched for dealing with edema, the swelling and inflammation that can be caused by arthritis, repetitive stress injuries, sports-related soreness, and many other issues. Malachite has a lot of the mineral copper in it, so a pendant, ring, or bracelet with malachite can be a great agent for pain reduction. Iron-rich magnetite is another pain absorber.

## CHAKRA CRYSTALS

The concept of chakras originated many thousands of years ago in Asia. The ancient philosophers and metaphysicians identified seven main energy centers around the body and saw each chakra emanating energy in the form of a rainbow color that affected the mental, physical, and spiritual balance in a human being. Chakra theory is the basis of many Eastern healing practices. One of the simplest ways to achieve well-being is to place crystals on the parts of the body where certain chakras are centered. Many people I know credit their clarity and well-being to chakra therapy. One sure way to relieve stress and fortify the emotional body is this laying on of crystals.

| Chakra | Color | Energies | Corresponding Crystals |
|---|---|---|---|
| First, root (base of spine) | red | security, survival | garnet, smoky quartz |
| Second, sacral | orange | pleasure | amber, carnelian |
| Third, solar plexus | yellow | drive, personal power | amber, citrine, topaz |
| Fourth, heart | green | abundance, love, serenity | peridot, rose quartz |
| Fifth, throat | blue | creativity, originality | blue quartz, tiger's-eye |
| Sixth, third eye | indigo | intuitiveness, perception | fluorite, lapis lazuli |
| Seventh, crown | violet | holy bliss, all is one | amethyst, diamond |

# COLORS AND SHAPES— CROSSING THE RAINBOW BRIDGE

The colors of stones, gems, and minerals have great meaning and are clues to the power lying within the crystalline structures. Color is one form of energy with individual vibrations. It is becoming common knowledge that the color in our work and home environments can affect our moods, calm us down, make us more energetic and more romantic, and promote any number of desired states of being. Decorators have to study psychology now! Whatever the case, anyone using color is, consciously or not, tuning in to the vibrational frequency of color.

The color system springs from seven basic vibrations, the same ones at the foundation of our chakra system and also the musical scale. The "heaviest"

**CRYSTAL BLISS**

If you want pleasant and divinely restful sleep and dreams, place these crystals under your mattress: moonstone, tiger's-eye, and turquoise.

---

vibrations are at the bottom, and the "lightest" vibrations are at the top. Each of the seven basic colors relates to one of the seven chakras. Highly skilled psychics can read your aura and see the energy radiating out from your body as colors. You can use color management on the simplest level each day of your life. If you wake up feeling depressed, wear yellow to raise your energy level. If you are having a big business meeting, do wear red, the power color. If you have a meeting with some folks and you want to put them at ease, by all means, wear the earthy colors of brown or green and you will see them relax with gratitude. When I need inspired ideas, I wear blue. And, like many other similar-minded folks, I wear purple when I want to be at my most spiritual.

Following is a guide to colors. Don't be afraid to really let go and work with a multitude of hues. Have fun, and remember how you feel while you are learning and experimenting. Find your soul colors!

**RED** relates to the root chakra and corresponds to security and survival issues. On a soul level, red is passion and intensity. On a healing level, it is warmth and fights cancer.

Subcolors of red are rose red (corresponding to issues regarding mother, home, grounding, and money; soulwise, it is love), clear red (corresponding to the sense of smell; soulwise, it is anger), and red orange (corresponding to sexual passion).

Red is the most physical of the colors and is also a strong emotional color. Red gems and crystals are the ones to aid you in matters of the body. Jasper, amber, and agate in shades of red can help people who have a hard time with shyness to feel stronger. It is of great interest to me that I am seeing a huge resurgence of interest in red coral. This stone is a great help to the skeleton and bones. I think people need to feel their vitality more than ever. Red coral is also a boost to the lungs, and there has been an increase in influenza, tuberculosis, and asthma such as we have not seen since the Depression era.

For the Chinese, red rice symbolizes immortality. In the tarot, the hermit, the high priestess, and the empress wear red beneath blue robes, symbolizing the great hidden knowledge they hold. Dark red relates to female mysteries and the source of all life.

**PINK** is a sweeter color and has a calmer vibration than the reds. Where red is passionate, pink is nurturing. Pink is the esteem-boosting color and can direct love to the self, which is very important in this day and age when people are so directed by others. Pink pearl will also make your intuition about love and romance more accurate. Those of us who pick the wrong people, could do well to sport a pink pearl ring or pendant. Pink coral makes for a sweet, upbeat, and more genuinely loving attitude. Rose quartz will help in self-enhancement and directing positive energy toward the self. Rhodonite, rhodochrosite, or a big pink diamond will help build an unconditionally positive regard within and without.

**ORANGE** relates to the sacral chakra, or abdominal region, and corresponds to physical urges such as hunger and sex. Soulwise, it is ambition. For healing, it helps with sexual issues, increases potency, and builds stronger immunity. Orange is great for stimulation and motivation; it hones and builds focused energy. Orange is also great for lucidity and orderliness. Carnelian, in the family of orange crystals, is the stone to wear if you are embarking on a new exercise regimen or training for a sporting event. Any orange stone will help keep the physical and emotional self in balance. Some parents have reported great effects after giving a child who was a finicky eater a carnelian to wear. If you are feeling a bit depressed or missing some of your general lust for life, do wear an orange stone. You will snap out of it right away!

The saffron orange robes of Buddhist monks reflect divine life, as do the orange velvet crosses of the Knights of the Holy Ghost. Roman brides wore vials of orange to indicate the eternalness of the wedding vows.

**YELLOW** relates to the solar plexus chakra and to personal power, freedom, control, fire, and the eyes. Soulwise, it rules the intellect. For healing, yellow is clarity. If you are in a career that necessitates good communication, place a big chunk of yellow quartz on your bookshelf in your office; this will create a cheerful energy and kindle your desire to be in contact. You should wear citrine, topaz, or yellow zircon to improve your ability to speak clearly and with ease. Or, if you are shy, yellow amber will help you to open up and share. These yellow stones will also make life more enjoyable for they are harbingers of happiness. Yellow is also a color that encourages honesty. Wearing yellow crystals as jewelry during your working day will help you and your coworkers on a daily basis.

**GREEN** relates to the heart chakra and to relationships, the heart and lungs, the element of air, the sense of touch, and the will for life. Soulwise, it is the caring nurturer and the healer. In healing, it helps with balance and general, overall health and well-being. Green stones are among the most beloved, and it is easy to see why because they offer so much emotional soothing. Emerald and green jade bring security, prosperity, and protection. Other green stones, such as chrysocolla and malachite, calm the mind, and green-flecked bloodstone is a stress buffer.

Alchemists taught that the light of the emerald revealed the most closely guarded of all secrets. In medieval times, physicians wore green cloaks as they worked with greens—herbs and simples—for curing. It is still the color preferred by pharmacologists. Green is the color associated with the wood element in Chinese astrology. For Muslims, green is the emblem of salvation. In medieval times, painters portrayed Christ's cross in green, as it was the instrument by which the human race was regenerated through his great sacrifice. Green stones have a large role in the Arthurian and Holy Grail legends.

**BLUE** relates to the throat chakra and to communication, intuition, listening, and the ears. Soulwise, blue is the teacher. For healing, it maintains calm and protects the aura. I have to admit to a preference, above all, for blue stones. I don't like them because I know blue is a mental color; I just have a natural attraction. We all need to pay attention to such affinities, as they express much about our psyches. Blue is the color of creativity and mind control. To embark on any creative and intellectually demanding project, try wearing a lovely ring or pendant of blue lace agate. If you are feeling like you might be obsessing over something or overly influenced by someone else's thoughts and opinions, try sodalite, one of the stones relegating independence of mind. Beautiful blue sapphire is also great for making personal declarations of independence and for feeling good about yourself while you make them.

To Tibetan Buddhists and to the Egyptians, the color blue has represented transcendent wisdom; it is truth. For Christians, blue and white are the colors of Mary, our Lady, and of detachment from the material world. In Poland, the houses of brides-to-be are painted blue.

**INDIGO** relates to the third eye and to intuition. Soulwise, it represents the urge toward the spiritual. For healing, it opens the third eye and promotes clearheadedness.

**VIOLET** relates to the crown chakra and connection to all else in the universe. Soulwise, it is the deep connection to spirit. For healing, it works on deep tissue and helps rid oneself of deep pain. Gentle purple amethyst is good for issues of sensitivity. Many people drink too much because they are sensitive to environmental noise and are trying to block out some of the overstimulation. Another reason for substance abuse is the longing for an ecstatic spiritual experience. Amethyst helps in all such instances and keeps your energy from draining out of you. The purplish agates will also guard the receptive nature and act as ballasts for stability and contentment. Violet is associated with secrecy, the veil behind which transformation takes place.

**BROWN, GRAY, BLACK, WHITE, SILVER, AND GOLD** are not chakra colors but certainly exist in the world of crystals and stones. Ancient Romans and the Catholic Church regarded brown as the color of humility and poverty—thus the brown robes for monastic orders. Brown is a color representing safety and the home. Brown gems and rocks are great stability stones for grounding. Agate, jasper, and petrified wood all act as agents of security.

The ancient Egyptians regarded gray as the color of fertility. The color symbolized resurrection in medieval times, and the artists of that era depicted Jesus at the Last Judgment in robes of gray, the color of grief and mourning. Gray, however, is the first color the human eye can perceive in infancy.

Black is about protection and strength. If you are surrounded by psychic vampires who rob your energy, wear jet or onyx or obsidian. This color also girds your personal energies and gives you more inner authority. In North Africa, black symbolizes the color of the life-giving rich earth and of nourishing rain clouds. Christian and Muslim clergy wear black robes to proclaim their renunciation of all vanity and show their faith. Sufi dervishes see the progress of the inner life as a ladder of color, starting at the lowest rung of white and ascending to the highly evolved black, the absolute color to which all other colors lead.

White represents purity, peace, patience, and protection; silver relates to communication and greater access to the universe; and gold is a direct connection to God and facilitates wealth and ease.

Combining your gems and crystals with certain metals is very meaningful. The metal mounting of your jewelry is a vessel that contains and supports the energy of the stone. There are five metals commonly used—gold, silver, and platinum are the precious metals, and brass and copper are the semiprecious metals.

# MANDALA

Raise your chi with crystal mandalas. A mandala is sacred space through which we can connect to the greater energy of the universe for spiritual growth and health and well-being. Different designs and grids have different properties. By laying out these sacred patterns, you can focus and calm yourself and create conscious change in your mind and body. The wheel with spokes is the most common pattern, but you should experiment and create your own new form with crystals and meditate upon it.

# LAYING ON OF STONES

This crystal-healing practice is distilled from the study of chakras. Here are just a few examples of how to apply crystals directly upon your body or that of anyone else who needs healing. After you have gotten the knack of it, you can use the information in this book to try your own applications of stones and gems.

The first step for anyone undertaking crystal healing is to lie down, relax, and get very comfortable. Empty everything else from your mind.

Lapis lazuli and its fellow blue aquamarine can be laid upon the throat chakra to release any blockage therein. This greatly aids in self-expression and is wonderful for professional speakers as well as performers such as actors and singers. Turquoise laid on the face—cheeks, forehead, and chin—is a calming agent, significantly reducing tension. Azurite on the brow opens the third eye and deepens wisdom; this can be a door opening to enlightenment.

Clear quartz crystal placed upon the brow, each cheek, and the chin can balance the energy of the head and allow more light into the third eye.

Malachite, a heart stone, placed near the heart and along the center of the abdomen will create a sense of harmony and facilitate letting go of pain, suffering, and old childhood wounds.

The Rainbow is a simple and effective method for total-body wellness. Choose from this list of stones, making sure you have one of each color of the rainbow—violet, indigo, blue, green, yellow, orange, and red—plus one white stone and one black stone for completion. Then, simply lay the stones on their corresponding chakra centers. I've included a list of crystal and body affinities in case there is any specific area you want to focus on:

+ **amber** for the thyroid,
+ **benitoite** for the pituitary,
+ **beryl** for the eyes,
+ **bloodstone** for the kidneys,
+ **blue tourmaline** for the thymus,
+ **brown jasper** for the shins and for the skin,
+ **calcite** for the skeletal system,
+ **carnelian** for the liver,
+ **celestite** for the intestines,
+ **chalcedony** for the spleen,
+ **chrysocolla** for the pancreas,
+ **chrysolite** for the appendix,
+ **chrysoprase** for the prostate,
+ **danburite** for the muscles,
+ **dendrite agate** for the nervous system,
+ **dioptase** for the lungs,
+ **fire agate** for the stomach,
+ **fluorite** for the teeth,
+ **garnet** for the spine,
+ **hematite** for the blood and circulatory system,
+ **jadeite** for the knees,
+ **lapis lazuli** for the throat,

- **magnetite** for the joints,
- **moldavite** for the hands,
- **moonstone** for the womb area,
- **orange calcite** for the bladder,
- **purple fluorite** for the bone marrow,
- **rose quartz** for the heart,
- **smoky quartz** for the feet,
- **topaz** for the male genitals.

# CRYSTAL MEDITATION

Crystals are tools used to heal and transform our lives. I think of them as the tools of the metaphysician. *Meta* means "beyond" or "above," and *physics* is the science of the physical world. So *metaphysics* literally means "beyond physics," and there is much that cannot be explained by ordinary science and the laws that have been established. Physics is very much about tracing energy and the origins and effects of it, yet ordinary science and physics cannot necessarily explain how crystals manage and direct energy in powerful ways. They can be used to store, change, amplify, focus, and send energy.

Crystals can be a point for focus, an aid to absolute clarity of thought and intention. I was once told that these stones can be "tuning forks" for the consciousness, a thought I just love.

I recommend this meditation exercise for training yourself to gain laser-like focus: Lie on the floor in a place where you will not be distracted. Clear your thoughts and open your mind. Place a small quartz in the center of your forehead. Your pineal gland is located here, as is your third eye—the source of all intuition. After a few moments pass, you should start to have visualizations that are sort of like daydreams, but these messages are from your higher consciousness. I have had friends and workshop mates report that while performing this technique they went into another realm entirely—a fantasy world, a paradise, an unknown and very appealing place. Nearly everyone reports that they passed through a set of gates. You should perform this meditation for about thirty minutes, but no longer. We don't want anyone to leave us for too long and remain in a reverie.

After you try meditating solo, you may want to participate in activities with a group. At a retreat I organized for Z Budapest at the Ralston White Retreat Center in Mill Valley, California, she led us through a truly magical journey deep into Mother Earth. This was for the purpose of grounding us so we could get the most benefit from the weekend adventure. With Z's permission, I will share this meditation with you. You can do it with a group of people who have a shared intention. Start by having everyone lie down in a circle formation with their eyes closed. Z's guided tour follows:

> *Blessed beings, you are about to enter the Mother, our great earth goddess, Gaia. In your mind, you are standing with bare feet on the ground. You can feel the grass with your toes, the solid earth underneath your feet. Feel the solidity and fastness of the earth fill your body with strength; we are all made of clay. We come from the death, and we are made of earth. Feel your connection to the Mother. We come from the earth, her womb. We are made of stardust and clay and the waters of the ocean. Feel the blood in your veins. The water of life. Know that you are alive. Feel her winds, the breath of life. Breathe deeply ten times, completely filling your lungs and completely emptying your lungs. Breathe and feel your chest rising and falling with each breath.*

*Now feel your backbone connecting to the earth; you feel a cord connecting you and your life to the earth. Concentrate on the cord until you can feel it running all the way through you and deep into the earth. Tug on the cord; feel it give. Now, take the cord in your hands and follow it down, down, deep into the earth. It is dark as you go down and down, but do not be frightened. Trust in the universe and keep descending into the bosom of the Mother. Down we go, not falling but moving purposefully, gracefully, following the cord of the earth. Now you see light. Keep moving toward the light and keep holding the cord as it leads you to the shining distance.*

*The light grows nearer, and you see that it is an opening, a cave, a safe place in which to shelter. Enter the cave. It is filled with light, firelight reflected off a thousand crystal points. An old woman sits at the fire, warming her bones in her warm and dry cave. It is beautiful, more beautiful than the palace of any king or the castle of any queen. It is the crystal cave of the Goddess, and you are with her. Show your respect to the Goddess and light the incense at her altar at the side of the cave, piled up with many shimmering stones and priceless gems, the bounty and beauty of our generous benefactor. Sit at her feet and take in her love, her power, and her grace. Sit quietly and hear the special message she has for you. You are her child, and she has dreamed a dream for you. Now we listen and breathe. Blessed be.*

Z led us back to the circle, and after that, nobody's life was ever the same. In my experience with this particular guided visualization, I could smell the incense as we lit it. All the women at this retreat had profound experiences with Z Budapest and the Goddess that day. It helped greatly to have such a skilled guide as the Dianic priestess Ms. Budapest, with her purring Hungarian accent. But with caring intention and the willingness to really let go, we can all achieve marvelous breakthroughs with these meditative exercises.

On that day, I received a very specific insight from the Goddess to go back to graduate school and pursue my abandoned dream of a master's degree in medieval studies. I felt exhilarated by this and resolute in my decision. I felt alive with purpose and so blessed to be pursuing both my scholarship and my spirituality. I remember that the reality of working full-time and going to school at night wasn't easy, but whenever I started to stumble on my path, I remembered back to the crystal cave and my time with the great and glowing Goddess in her magnificent crystal cave, and I immediately felt stronger.

Here is an exercise I learned long ago from my mentor in all things magical, Z Budapest, for the transformation of energy: Fill a bowl with 2 cups of water, preferably distilled or, better yet, good old rainwater. Put a chunk of clear quartz crystal that weighs at least 6 ounces into the water basin. Take another bowl of the same size and fill it with the exact same kind of water and place it in another room at least 15 feet away from the bowl containing the crystal. After one full day and night, fill two glasses with the water from each bowl; you will marvel at the difference in taste. What makes the difference? There is a molecular change in the water containing the crystal. The water is transformed.

## *Tips 'n' Tricks*

### CRYSTAL CLOSURE

If you are having a hard time getting away from a relationship that you feel isn't good for you any longer, get closure by wearing morganite until the other person gets the message.

# CRYSTAL VISUALIZATION

Crystals are also powerful amplifiers. Berry, another priestess in Z's circle, taught me that crystals store and back up our thoughts. She pointed out that it is very important to clear out any thoughts of negativity when working with crystals, as many can store this bad energy and emanate it in all directions. She taught me to be clear in my thinking when working with crystals so that all influences would be both positive and good. You see, crystals affect the energy of the body as well as the energy of the mind.

Berry showed me a technique for measuring this amplification. She had me choose two seedlings; I chose two tomato plants of the same size. Then, I was instructed to treat the plants exactly the same way in terms of water, light, and food. I placed the same quartz crystal I used in the water-transformation test beside the left tomato seedling, which I placed 4 feet apart from the other seedling. When I tended the plants each day, I gave them exactly the same basic necessities, but Berry instructed me to take the crystal beside the leftmost seedling and hold it in my left hand while talking to the plant. It felt a bit silly at first, I admit. But soon, it became the most natural thing in the world to speak with the tomato plant and tell it what a wonderful tomato plant it was and how excited I would be to eventually taste its fruit. Also, I visualized it growing hearty and strong and loaded with tomatoes ripening for salad. Perhaps the most important step in the process was to send positive thought energy to the seedling. The seedling on the right received no daily chats or crystal vibes. After a month, you could tell an enormous difference. Both plants were healthy, but the plant on the left was much bigger and bushier. The crystal had clearly amplified the energy.

Crystals are not only used in batteries; they *are* batteries in their own right. Crystals become charged with energy and store that energy. Some crystal gazers also believe we can store information in crystals. The shamanic crystal skulls of the Mayans have caused people who have handled them to have many dreams and visions that seemed to be recordings of historic events. These crystal skulls are theorized to be depositors of all the knowledge of the Mayans—crude computers, if you will.

Again, using crystals to store energy must be approached mindfully and with great consciousness. If you are very happy one day, remember to pour some of that bliss into a crystal, and it will remain there as a source for some happiness on a blue day. Do not send negative energy into a crystal, as it will store the bad along with the good and be a negativity transmitter.

Very advanced crystal wielders also use crystal batteries for transferal of energy and even for telepathy, which, I must confess, goes well beyond my skill level.

# AN INTEGRATIVE APPROACH

I believe one of the primary reasons crystals populate our planet is for healing. I was a bit oblivious to this wonderful gift from the universe until I faced a serious health crisis of my own. Now, I am keenly interested in the healing power of crystals, and I am quite amazed at the extensive array of curatives crystals offer. However, do not ever replace traditional medicine with a crystal-only approach. If this sounds like a disclaimer, it most certainly is. I believe a combination of Eastern and Western medicine, inclusive of gem and crystal healing, is the best way to cover all of your bases for health and wellness. I believe that gem-healing magic can be the difference between feeling okay and feeling GREAT. And, who doesn't want to feel wonderful?

Part Two

# YOUR ULTIMATE
# GUIDE TO GEMS

This half of the book is your ultimate resource guide. It is, in fact, the mother lode! This extensive reference to rocks, gems, and crystals has descriptions of the origins, magical qualities, and mythologies of all the great gems, common and uncommon crystals, and some very rare rocks. This information is intended to guide you through your own explorations of what you need for spells and health improvements, and what stones suit your personality and whims. Peruse this section when you are thinking about which jewelry to wear and which crystals to keep at home and at work for an altogether radiant you.

# Chapter Seven

# GEM
# MYTHOLOGY

One of the most fascinating legends involving gems and crystals is about the lost island of Atlantis. While hundreds of books have been written about this great mystery, only a few key authors talked about the use of crystals on Atlantis. The great Edgar Cayce, psychic extraordinaire, reported much information on the topic. In her book *The World Before,* Ruth Montgomery explained the use of crystals by the people of Atlantis and another mysterious lost civilization, Lemuria. Taylor Caldwell, at the tender age of 12, wrote a book entitled *Romance of Atlantis,* in which she described sensory memories of Atlanteans working with crystals for rejuvenation and then living, in some cases, for hundreds of years!

Much of this information is channeled, coming through almost as though it were "downloaded" into the receiver's consciousness. I find this interesting and take it with one or two grains of salt, but I do have a Beat writer friend, Eileen Kaufman, who has very distinct memories of her past life on Atlantis. Eileen remembers being a priestess who tried to warn of the coming cataclysm to no avail. She told me that I was there, too, along with another friend who has since passed away. She said it was a tsunami that swept everyone away. When she relayed her crystal-clear memories about our life in Atlantis, I felt a stirring of ancient memory, and it just felt right. I know she was telling me something very true from long ago. Suddenly, it even made sense to me that I was so fascinated with ancient civilizations as a child and wanted to be an archaeologist for as long as I can remember. I even wrote a little book when I was 12 called the *Excavation of Troy*.

This much I know is true: There are things that go beyond any understanding, and they require our trust in the universe. Atlantis is one of them. We have much to learn about who we are as humans, where we come from, and where we are going. My mantra has become "I trust in the future. I trust in the universe."

Here is a brief history of Atlantis based on what I have read and on the dreams and memories of the wise and wonderful Eileen Kaufman.

The people of Atlantis were powerful and fairly advanced for their time, slightly prior to the golden age of Greece. They used crystal technology, merging the mind with machines. They also used these crystals as solar-power generators, and everyone had access to this wonderful and completely free source of electricity. They used huge lenses, both concave and convex, to gather the energy and store it in a liquid crystal solution. The Atlanteans also utilized crystals in an enormous grid to capture the energy of the earth. They "grew" massive crystals in very specific shapes and were very sophisticated about using them in transportation, architecture, agriculture, industry, medicine, and psychic work.

The people of Atlantis were very spiritual and built many temples filled with crystals. Their priests and priestesses were also healers who developed the use of crystals into an art. Sadly, as the legend goes, the crystal power was corrupted by a handful of folks who abused it, using it not for the greater good but for personal gain. There was said to be a cataclysmic release of energy that caused an imbalance in the earth underneath Atlantis, resulting in a massive earthquake and tsunami that destroyed the civilization forever.

I like to think of this partially as a parable about the wise use of crystals or any tools of magic. It must be for the greater good, and the user must be conscious. Harm to none!

## AMETHYST—*the Rose de France*

The Chinese have been wearing amethyst for more than 8,000 years. Tibetans consider this stone to be sacred to Buddha and make prayer beads from it. One lovely legend associated with the purple crystal is that it comes from Bacchus, the Greek god of wine. Mere mortals had angered this divinity, and he vowed a violent death—death by tiger—to the very next mortal he would encounter. A pretty girl by the name of Amethyst was en route to the worship at the temple of Diana. The goddess Diana protected Amethyst by turning her into clear crystal quartz so she could not be torn apart by the ravaging tiger. Bacchus regretted his actions and anointed Amethyst with his sacred wine. However, he didn't pour enough to cover her entirely, leaving her legs without color. Thus, amethyst is usually uneven in its purple color. The fact that Amethyst was anointed with wine also relates to the healing power of this stone to help with sobriety. The Greek word *amethystos* means "without wine." In the Victorian era, a paler amethyst was called Rose de France and was a favorite stone in jewelry. The Victorians sometimes left amethysts out in the sun to fade them. Nowadays, the darker purple stones are considered much more valuable.

## AQUAMARINE—*Seawater Stone*

A favorite among sailors and mariners, this stone is said to keep them safe. Aquamarine is the signifier of the oceanic divinities, sea goddesses and sirens. The Egyptians loved this gem and gifted it to the dead as part of the treasure hoard to grant them safety in the next life. They also gifted it to the gods of the netherworld as a guarantee of safe passage. Egyptian high priests wore on their shoulders two aquamarines, or shoham, as they called them, engraved with the names of the six tribes of Egypt. This sacred stone was also one of the twelve sanctified gems used in the breastplate of the biblical King Solomon. Today, aquamarine can be a boon to a couple, as it helps maintain a long and happy marriage. And it defends against the devil! The sun is the nemesis of the blue gem because the color of aquamarine fades if overexposed to sunlight.

## BERYL—*Stone of Power*

Medieval historian Arnoldus Saxo said that warriors used beryl to help in battle and also reported that it was good for court cases. Saxo was perhaps a bit hyperbolic in his declaration that the wearer of this stone was made unconquerable and smarter and cured of any laziness! Thomas de Cantimpre's German classic *De Proprietatibus Rerum* spoke about the power of the stone beryl to reawaken the love of married couples. Early crystal balls were frequently made of beryl polished into spheres, rather like J. R. R. Tolkien's palantirs used by wizards. The Druids and Celts used beryl to divine the future, and legend has it that Merlin, King Arthur's magician, carried a beryl ball around with him for exactly that purpose.

## BLOODSTONE—*Martyr's Stone*

In medieval times, Christians used bloodstone for sculptured bas-reliefs depicting the martyred saints and Christ's crucifixion—thus the name "martyr's stone." The myth behind bloodstone is that some of Christ's blood dripped down and stained jasper that lay at the foot of the cross. In the great Louvre Museum, in Paris, is the seal of Holy Roman Emperor Rudolf II carved into bloodstone. The ancient Egyptians loved bloodstone and gifted it to pharaohs, great warriors, and kings, believing it had the power to calm their tempers and prevent wrath and bloodshed.

An ancient book of Egyptian magic, known as *The Leyden Papyrus,* recorded the high regard for bloodstone: "The world has no greater thing; if any one have this with him he will be given whatever he asks for; it also assuages the wrath of kings and despots, and whatever the wearer says will be believed. Whoever bears this stone, which is a gem, and pronounces the name engraved upon it, will find all doors open while bonds and stone walls will be rent asunder."

Damigeron, a classical historian, wrote that bloodstone could disclose the future through what were called audible oracles and could also change the weather. He further claimed that this favored stone kept the mind sharp and the body healthy and protected the reputation of anyone who wore it.

## CALCITE—*Bone of the Earth*

The ancients believed that calcite placed at the base of a pyramid could amplify the structure's power.

## CARNELIAN—*Safety Stone*

Said the ancient Egyptian religious leader Jafar, "He who wears carnelian will have whatever he desires." Wearing carnelian dates back to at least biblical times; there are several mentions of soldiers and priests wearing it. Carnelian was a favorite in ancient and medieval times, when people believed that wearing the stone could protect them against injury from falling stones. As the saying goes, "No man who wore a carnelian was ever found in a collapsed house or beneath a fallen wall." Other lore of this jewel includes the Armenian belief that an elixir of powdered carnelian would lift any cloud to life and fill the heart with happiness. In olden days, carnelian was credited with being able to defy no less than the devil! So, people wore this lovely red-orange stone with the intention of protecting themselves from evil, oftentimes repeating this prayer:

> *"In the name of God the Just, the very Just!*
> *I implore you, O God, King of the World,*
> *God of the World,*

*Deliver us from the Devil*
*Who tries to do harm and evil to us*
*Through bad people and from the evil of the envious."*

## CELESTITE—*Angel Stone*

Use this stone to get in contact with your guardian angel. The lore about this sky blue stone is that it is a star seed from the Pleiades and that those 100 million geodes were sent to Earth. It is a truth-telling crystal, rendering anyone holding it unable to tell lies.

Angelite is a condensed form of celestite with a highly unusual pattern of striping that looks like angel wings. Both forms of the magical stone will put you in touch with spirits and helpful energies from the angelic realm.

## CHALCEDONY—*Stone of Protection*

Chalcedony, made of Earth's ancient living things, has incredible powers of protection. In the eighteenth century, it was used to chase off bogeymen or anything that went bump in the night. Associated with the Holy Grail, chalcedony was a favorite material for chalices and was believed to provide protection even from poison.

## CHRYSOPRASE—*Love of Truth*

Emanuel Swedenborg, a seventeenth-century Swedish theologian, scientist, philosopher, and metaphysician, credited this apple-green chalcedony with giving people a love of the truth. Other lore regarding chrysoprase is that the stone offers a most rare capability to give a man set to be hanged a sure escape from his executioner. All he has to do, supposedly, is place this crystal in his mouth.

## DIAMONDS—*Fragments of the Stars*

I love the charming legend that Europeans first discovered diamonds from Africa in the pouch of a shaman, who used them for healing magic. Prehistoric peoples believed they were fragments of the stars and teardrops of the gods. In the most ancient times, diamonds were worn simply as adornment in their unpolished and rough state. As you might easily guess, diamonds are thought to bring luck, but there is another school of thought purported by diamondphobes who believe that these gems bring sure misfortune. The legend of the Hope diamond is a fascinating history wherein every owner of the royal rock was bankrupted until it was nestled in the safe of the Smithsonian Institution in Washington, D.C.

Diamonds are associated with lightning and with ensuring victory to warriors wearing them. Diamonds are thought to be powerful enough to fend off madness and even to stave off the devil himself! The medieval mystic Rabbi Benoni believed that diamonds were conducive to true spiritual joy and had power over the very stars and planets in the heavens.

A curiosity regarding most of the lore about diamonds is that they are supposed to be effective only if received as gifts; the outright purchase of a diamond is said to ruin the magic. I don't agree on this; if I could afford a diamond for myself, I *know* it would bring me enormous fortune!

Renaissance astrologer and scholar Gerolamo Cardano was wary of the crown jewel of crown jewels. He proclaimed this about the diamond: "It is believed to make the wearer unhappy; its effects therefore are the same upon the mind as that of the sun upon the eye, for the latter rather dims than strengthens the sight. It indeed engenders fearlessness, but there is nothing that contributes more to our safety than prudence and fear; therefore it is better to fear." Alchemist

Pierre de Boniface was far more confident about this queen of crystals, claiming it could render anyone wearing one invisible! Still, other medieval healers and humbugs claimed diamonds could cure poisoning and were themselves a powerful poison if ground up. Perhaps the most obvious unfounded claim regarding diamonds is that they could overcome and cure the plague.

## EMERALDS—*Popular Protectors*

Emeralds are believed to have been brought to Earth from the planet Venus. This precious stone is one of the only ones that retains its value, according to gemologists and jewelers, even if it is deeply flawed. Emeralds have a richly varied mythology attached to their glowing green history. For thousands of years, Hindu physicians in India regarded this stone as a benefit to many stomach-related illnesses—it was an appetite stimulant, a curative for dysentery, a laxative, and a treatment for too much stomach-irritating bile. In India of old, they also believed emeralds could drive away demons or rid a body of ill spirits.

Another antiquated belief about emeralds is that they portended events from the future, rather like scrying, or seeing things in a mirror or the glassy surface of the gem. Emeralds were thought to be foes to sorcerers, a belief stemming from a legend that emeralds vanquished all wizardry in their wake. The ancients loved emeralds and connected them with the eyes. Theophrastus, a student of Plato's, taught that emeralds protected the eyesight. He was taken so seriously that engravers kept emeralds on their tables to look at to refresh their eyes.

Egyptians valued emeralds almost beyond any other stone and claimed their goddess, Isis, wore a great emerald. Anyone who looked upon Isis's green jewel was assured of a safe trip to the underworld, the land of the dead. Egypt was the main source for emeralds until the sixteenth century. The Cleopatra mines, south of Cairo, were the mother lode, and emerald traders from as far away as India sought the stones, obtained at great human cost under wretched conditions of extreme heat and dangerous underground shafts. I hope the common belief that these stones also protected people from any poison and all venomous serpents was true here. Emeralds were anathemas to snakes, which would supposedly be struck blind by merely looking upon the stones.

In ancient Rome, emeralds were quite sought after by the wealthy class. Nero watched the games in the Colosseum through a set of priceless spectacles made from emeralds. However, with the capture of South America by Pizarro and Cortés, the Spanish in the 1500s made emeralds more available to the Europeans, who had an insatiable appetite for jewels and gold. The discovery in 1558 of the Muzo mine in Colombia uncovered emeralds of incredible beauty and size, prompting the Spanish conquistadors to take over the mine and declare the natives slaves. Perhaps part of Montezuma's revenge involved the seizure of the emerald mines. Emeralds were a popular cure for dysentery in the sixteenth century when worn touching the torso or held in the mouth. As with all very valuable stones, the people who actually mine them have no access to them unless they are smuggled out of the mines. According to a recent article in *National Geographic,* however, this is done more frequently than one might think, especially with larger stones. "Almost every high-quality emerald was smuggled at some point in its history," according to *National Geographic.*

## GARNET—*Noah's Lantern*

Garnets have much lore around them. The ancients believed them to have protective powers that prevented travelers from accidents and mishaps and also kept the sleeping from nightmares and bad dreams. It is said that the fiery glow of a garnet kept Noah and his ark afloat. A popular biblical gem, garnet was one of the stones used by King Solomon in his breastplate. In Asia, garnets were used as bullets, most notably in the rebellion in India in 1892. Garnet's name comes from the Greek word for pomegranate, and the gem is associated with a Greek myth surrounding this fruit. Persephone, the daughter of Zeus and Demeter, tasted three seeds from the pomegranate, dooming herself to spend half of the year in the underworld, married to Hades, god of the underworld.

## IRON PYRITE—*Fool's Gold*

Iron pyrite was supreme in early Mexico, where it was polished into mirrors for shamanic scrying, a method of looking into the future and the past. These people also carved sacred symbols into these vessels of interdimensional viewing.

## JADE—*The Concentrated Essence of Love*

Jade has been called the concentrated essence of love. The French literary legend Voltaire, author of *Candide,* was involved in a kidney-stone scandal caused by the innocent generosity of a Mademoiselle Paulet, who gave Voltaire a lovely jade bracelet. She wanted him to be cured in the same way she had, but French society thought it was a token of love, and his reputation was irrevocably damaged.

I always thought jade was a word of Asian origin until I learned better. It comes from the Spanish word *piedra de hijada,* translating to "stone of the flank," a name prompted by the Indian use of jade as a cure for kidney disease. Jade also served as an aid to ancient midwives and birth mothers, and on the opposite end of the spectrum of life, the Egyptians, Chinese, and Mayans placed a small piece of jade into the mouths of the dead.

The erudite world-exploring nobleman Sir Walter Raleigh wrote this about jade: "These Amazones have likewise great stores of these plates of gold, which they recover by exchange, chiefly for a kind of greene stone, which the Spaniards call Piedras Hijada, and we use for spleene stones and for the disease of the stone we also esteem them. Of these I saw divers in Guiana, and commonly every King or Casique had one, which theire wife for the most part weare, and they esteeme them as great jewels."

## JASPER—*Building Block of Heaven*

According to the Bible, the top of the holy walls of New Jerusalem, or heaven, contain 4,780 bricks encrusted with 1,327 hand-cut, polished red jasper stones. Jasper is mentioned throughout the Bible, particularly as a protective stone in the breastplates of the priests of Aaron. Evidently, the ancients considered it to be an extremely powerful stone. Even God is referred to metaphorically as a red jasper stone in one interpretation of Revelation chapter 4, verse 3, which states, "And He who sat there was like a jasper and a sardius stone in appearance; and there was a rainbow around the throne, in appearance like an emerald." (NKJV, www.Biblelight.org)

The ancients also favored jasper for curing snakebites, repelling evil spirits, and controlling the weather by bringing rain. "Lithica," a fourth-century epic poem, praises this stone: "The gods propitious hearken to his prayers, who'ever the polished glass-green Jasper wears: His parsed glebe they'll saturate with rain, and send for shower to soak the thirsty plain."

## LAPIS LAZULI—*Babylonian Blue*

Ancient Babylonians and their south-of-the-Mediterranean neighbors, the Egyptians, could not get enough of this bright blue jewel. The Egyptians named it chesbet and usually included it on their list of VIP items to be paid to nations under the dominion of the great kingdom of the Nile. The Babylonians, who piled lapis lazuli high in their tributes to Egypt, had access to a plenitude of this stone because they were the earliest people to mine it—back in 4000 B.C.!

Lapis lazuli was so holy to the Egyptians that the high priest himself wore a pendant of the blue stone in the shape of their goddess of truth, Mat. The Egyptians seemingly wished to swim in seas of lapis, as they used it daily—as adornment, for funeral masks and tools, and as an ingredient in their art, traditions that lasted for many generations into the future. Lapis has the unusual ability to hold its pigment even when it is ground up, which leads to what is perhaps my favorite of all the myriad and wonderful uses of lapis lazuli: eye makeup. Can you imagine getting ready for a big night out by painting your eyelids peacock blue with a very expensive lapis lazuli—laced eye shadow? I love the idea, and I'm sure Cleopatra did, too.

## MAGNETITE—*Herculean Stone*

The ancients were fascinated with magnetite and its mysterious workings. The great Pliny wrote that the first instance of the discovery of magnetite, commonly known as lodestone, happened when a Cretan shepherd was walking on Mount Ida with his flock, and the nails of his shoes clung to a rock in the field. The shepherd's name was Magnes. Pliny also recorded the tale of Ptolemy, who wished to make an iron statue of a woman for a temple dedicated to his wife and his sister. The trick was that he wanted to use the new art of magnetism to suspend the statue in air without any visible means of support! Unfortunately for us, Ptolemy and his architect, the Alexandrian Dinocrates, died before its completion. Otherwise, there might have been an eighth wonder of the world.

Lodestone, the polarized version of magnetite, was held to be a protection against spells and other magical mischief. The ancients also believed that a small piece of lodestone beneath the pillow would be a testimony to virtue. Alexander the Great gave his soldiers lodestone to defend against unseen evil spirits.

## MALACHITE—*Stone of Juno*

This stripy green stone belonged to the Greek goddess Venus. The Greeks believed it had major magical powers when set in copper jewelry. The Romans switched things around a bit and turned malachite over to Juno, cutting it into triangular shapes to indicate her sacred peacock symbol. My favorite bit of malachite lore is that drinking from a goblet cut from this stone supposedly gave the imbiber understanding of the language of animals!

## MOONSTONE—*Prophecy and Passion*

In olden times, it was believed that wearing a moonstone during the waning moon would offer prophetic abilities. The people of India have held moonstone as holy for thousands of years, but they had a superstition against displaying the sacred stone except on a cloth of yellow, the most spiritual color in their culture. The Indians also believed moonstone was very potent in the bedroom and not only aroused enormous passion but also gave lovers the ability to read their future together. The only problem was that they had to hold the moonstone in their mouths during the full moon to enjoy these magical properties.

## OPAL—*Cupid's Stone*

In the classical era, humans believed that opals were pieces of rainbows that had fallen to the ground. They also dubbed this exquisite iridescent gem Cupid's stone because they felt it looked like the love god's skin. The Arabs believed opals fell from heaven in bright flashes of lightning, thus gaining their amazing fire and color play. The Romans saw opals as symbols of purity and optimism. They believed this stone could protect people from diseases. The Roman name for opal is so beautiful and evocative—*cupid paederos,* meaning "a child as beautiful as love."

Saint Albert the Great was one of the most learned men of the thirteenth century, a student of the natural sciences as well as theology, literature, and languages. He fancied mineralogy and waxed on about the opal: "The porphanus is a stone which is in the crown of the Roman Emperor, and none like it has ever been seen; for this very reason it is called porphanus. It is of a subtle vinous tinge, and its hue is as though pure white snow flashed and sparkled with the color of bright, ruddy wine and was overcome by this radiance. It is a translucent stone, and there is a tradition that, formerly, it shone in the nighttime, but now, in our age, it does not sparkle in the dark, it is said to guard the regal honor."

Opals had many superstitions attached to them. There was the belief that an opal wrapped in a bay-laurel leaf could cure any eye disease and combat weak hearts and infection. In the Middle Ages, opal was called *ophthalmios,* or "eye stone." The great Scandinavian epic the *Edda* contained verses about a stone forged by the smithy of the gods to form the eyes of children, doubtless a reference to opal. In olden days, it was thought that an opal would change color according to the mood and health of the owner, going dull and colorless when the owner died. Blond women favored opals because they believed they could keep their hair light in color. (I trust they were not using black or dark blue opals!)

It was even believed that an opal could render the wearer invisible, making this the patron stone of thieves. Black opal has always had top ranking among opals, being the rarest and the most dramatic type. One legend told that if a love relationship was consummated with one party wearing a black opal, the gem would soak up the passion and store it in its glow.

## PEARLS—*Tears of the Gods*

Pearls have a romantic past. The Chinese regarded them as the physical manifestation of the souls of oysters. One of the prettier names given to the pearl was *margarithe,* meaning "child of light." The Arabs called them tears of the gods and said they were formed when raindrops fell into oyster shells. In India, pearls were the perfect wedding gift, promising devotion and fertility. A Hindu wedding ritual involved the piercing of the perfect pearl, a virginity ceremony.

One less-than-successful cure for the plague was this ancient recipe: six grains of powdered pearl in water mixed with ash-tree sap. One remedy for excessive bleeding was a glass of water with one part burned pearl-powder. Snuffing the same was a treatment for headaches. Pearl oil was used for nervous conditions, and pearl poultice was even used for leprosy! Other less glamorous uses for pearl potions were treatments for hemorrhoids and poisoning. An elixir made with one-half of a pearl grain was supposed to cure impotence and be an overall aphrodisiac. In bygone days, people were so fond of grinding up pearls that they even used them in toothpaste!

## PERIDOT—*Pele's Teardrop*

Peridot is one of the most misunderstood gems on the planet. It is really a combination of two other stones, fayalite and forsterite, with a bit of iron, a dash of nickel and a pinch of chromium. The world's oldest source of the green charmer was the mist-shrouded desert island of Zerberget, also called Saint John's Island, off Egypt's coast. Unfortunately for the peridot miners, this island was a pit of deadly, venomous snakes! The pharaohs so treasured their peridot that any uninvited visitors to the island were put to death. Nowadays, the only residents of Zerberget are a few turtles and some seabirds. Perhaps the stones from the breastplate of Solomon and his high priest, Aaron, came from this odd little island. Peridot was one of the twelve stones believed to have the power to create miracles for the rituals of these priests and to help protect them in battle. Furthermore, Solomon drank soma (an intoxicating plant juice) from cups carved from peridot, thus gaining his wealth of wisdom.

Now that the mines on Zeberget are no more, most peridot is mined by Native Americans in Arizona and in the exotic locales of Myanmar, Sri Lanka, and the Kashmir Himalayas. Peridot has also been found in some meteorites. In the 1920s, a farmer in Kansas awoke one day to find lumps of peridot-studded meteorite in his fields. Maybe you really have to follow the peridot road to get to Oz!

It is believed that Cleopatra, queen of the Nile, adorned herself with high-quality peridots instead of emeralds. The Romans called peridot the evening emerald. The stone, brought back as booty by the Knights Templars and Crusaders, was used to adorn cathedrals in medieval times. On the Shrine of the Three Magi in Germany's Cologne Cathedral, there is a huge 200-carat peridot.

The powers of peridot are believed to be twice as intense if it is set in gold. Peridot was thought to have the power to drive away evil, and if you are so lucky as to have a goblet carved out of peridot, any medicine you might drink out of it will have magical healing powers. In Hawaii, the lore of this gem is that the goddess Pele cried tears that turned into peridots.

## RUBY—*Mother of the Earth's Blood*

In the tenth century, Chinese gem carvers engraved depictions of dragons and snakes on the surfaces of rubies to gain money and power. In India, worshippers gave rubies as an offering to their god Krishna, and in China, the stones paid homage to Buddha.

In his famed *Lapidary,* Philippe de Valois lavished praise on the royally red rock, writing that "the books tell us the beautiful clear and fine ruby is the lord

of stones; it is the gem of gems and surpasses all other precious stones in virtue."
Sir John Mandeville similarly evoked his opinion that ownership of a ruby would accord safety from all peril and wonderful relations with friends and neighbors. He further recommended that rubies be worn on the left side of the body.

In Myanmar, ruby was viewed as a stone of invincibility, and soldiers had a radical approach to harnessing its protective power—before marching into battle, they would embed the gem in their skin! They believed the color "ripened" inside the earth. Prehistoric peoples believed that rubies were crystallized drops of the mother of the earth's blood.

## SAPPHIRE—*Eye of Horus*

The ancient Persians believed that Earth rested on a giant sapphire and the blue sky was a reflection of its color. The Greeks identified white sapphire with the god Apollo. They deemed this stone very important indeed: The oracles at Delphi used it to make their prophecies. The Egyptians designated sapphire as the eye of Horus. Star sapphire is especially prized, as the lines crossing the blue of the stone were believed to represent faith, hope, and charity.

Sapphire has been used as an eye cure for millennia. Medieval scientist Sir Albert the Great recorded incidents in which he had seen sapphire used with success as a healer, stating that it was necessary for the stone to be dipped in cold water prior to surgery and afterward, as well. A contemporary of Albert the Great's by the name of von Helmont advocated using sapphire as a remedy for plague boils by rubbing the gem on the afflicted spots. He did offer the disclaimer that the condition could not be too advanced and explained the science behind his cure with the early theory of magnetism, in which a force in the sapphire pulled "the pestilential virulence and contagious poison from the infected part."

Part of the myth and magic of sapphires is that they offer a great deal of myth and magic. Magicians and seers love this stone because it adds to their sensitivities and enables them to augur better. Historically, it was regarded as a gem of nobility, and any regal personage wearing this noble gem would be protected from harm, particularly the threat of poison. Another dubious legend is that Moses wrote the Ten Commandments on tables of sapphire, but it is more likely that they would have been carved into the soft and more readily available lapis lazuli. Even with God on his side, where would Moses have gotten sapphires of such massive size and flatness? Sapphire remained popular with the religious; one notable instance was when the twelfth-century bishop of Rennes commend-ed this gem as an ecclesiastical ring due to its obvious connection to the heavens above. The holy- and legal-minded also favored this stone as it was believed to help counteract deception. Once, sapphires were believed to have gender. Dark sapphires were "male," and light stones were "female."

## STAR SAPPHIRE—*Giver of Great Luck*

Sir Richard Burton always carried a star sapphire with him as his talisman while he traveled through Asia and the Middle East. According to Burton, the stone brought him excellent horses and ensured that he received attention right when he needed it. It does seem to have worked, as he is still receiving accolades and consideration long after his passing. A generous soul, he would show his star sapphire to the friendly folk who had helped him, since this gem is a giver of great luck.

## TOPAZ—*Saint Hildegard's Cure*

Sailors once used this golden gem to shed light on the water during moonless nights. Topaz was also used as an aphrodisiac and to prevent the excesses of love, functions that certainly don't seem to go together. Ground into a dust and mixed with rose water, topaz was used to treat excessive bleeding. Similarly, powdered topaz mixed with wine was a treatment for insanity once upon a time. The ancients used topaz to guard against magicians by setting it in a gold bracelet and wearing it on the left arm. Saint Hildegard of Bingen, who suggested topaz was an aid to poor vision, placed the stone in wine for three straight days and then gently rubbed it on the eye. The wine could then be drunk—after removing the stone, of course. This is one of the first written records of a gem elixir. Medieval physicians also used topaz to treat the plague and its accompanying sores, and several miracles were attributed to a particular stone that had been in the possession of Pope Clement VI and Pope Gregory II.

## TURQUOISE—*Turkish Stone*

One pretty legend relating to turquoise is that it is generated by rainbows touching the earth. Turquoise seems to have always had a mythic link to horses, beginning with the medieval belief that anyone wearing this stone would be protected from falling off the animal. Sir John Mandeville's *Lapidaire* further claimed that this blue-green stone prevented horses from the harm of drinking cold water when they were sweating and hot. Turkish equestrians went so far as to attach this crystal to the bridles of their horses as a talisman for the animals.

An unusual story about turquoise comes from the court of Emperor Rudolph II, whose physician was given a specimen that had faded completely. The doctor's father had given it to him with these words of wisdom, "Son, as the virtues of the turquoise are said to exist only when the stone has been given, I will try its efficacy by bestowing it upon thee." The young man set it in a ring and in one month's time, the splendid color was completely restored.

## ZIRCON—*Legacy of Hyacinth*

Blue zircon is a thread of the fabric of Greek mythology. In the tale of the Greek youth Hyacinth, a blue hyacinth flower grew in the place where he died. In a less charming but equally fascinating fable, zircon was used for exorcism. The methodology was simple—a cross was cut into a loaf of freshly baked wheat bread. Then, a zircon was used to trace along the cross shape before the bread was eaten to drive away the evil spirits.

*Chapter Eight*

# GEM
# AND CRYSTAL
# DESCRIPTIONARY

## ABALONE

Abalone is the beautifully iridescent lining of a seashell—a product of our oceans and the end result of a living thing. Abalone is fished in California and in the warm, tropical coastal waters of Japan, China, and South America. Abalone is used to heal the heart and the muscle tissue, and to aid digestion. Use abalone as a dish to hold your sage smudging-stick for clearing energy at home. This gorgeous organic gem is a beautiful and sacred token for your altar or shrine at home. Just looking at abalone gives a sense of inner peace.

## AGATE

Agate, which comes from the chalcedony group of stones, was beloved by Egyptians for its side-by-side stripes. These stripes occur because of tiny crystals lined up in bands. Agate has a translucent quality and is found all over the world. It is used for grounding and balance and is said to enable higher consciousness. Agate is a stone of confidence and can make the wearer feel a better sense of self and engender more self-understanding. An agate necklace or ring is a powerful centering stone to wear at important meetings or presentations.

Botswana agate is named for the region in which it is found. Botswana agate is gray in color and looks smooth and waxy. This is a powerful tool for anyone dealing with smoke—whether a firefighter or a smoker who wants to quit the habit. Botswana agate is good for the skin, the lungs, and the respiratory system and can also fight depression.

Moss agate is usually a dark color: brown, black, or blue. Moss agate comes from India, North America, or Australia. It is named as such because it has patterning in light-colored clusters that resembles moss. This is a cleansing stone and can bring balance to both sides of the brain, therefore reducing depression or emotional ailments. Moss agate is also useful for treating hypoglycemia. It is the stone of farmers, botanists, and midwives—those who work with the earth. It also aids intuition and creativity and can reduce inhibition and shyness. If you are a speaker, singer, or performer who occasionally suffers stage fright, moss agate is your gem to wear.

## ALBITE

This is the rough sister of the polished moonstone. A milky-colored stone with blue shading, it can be found in Africa, Europe, and the Americas. Albite is helpful for immune system and breathing problems and can assist the spleen and thyroid. This translucent stone calms the wearer and fights depression. A chunk of albite in your bedroom will help banish the blues.

## ALEXANDRITE

First found in the 1800s in Russia, this stone was named after the country's czar, Alexander. It has since been found in Brazil and Sri Lanka. A mysterious green, alexandrite shines red under light. The phrase "emerald by day, ruby by night" illustrates the color changes of alexandrite. This stone can be of very great value and command a great price if the colors are pure. Alexandrite is good for the nerves and is calming to the wearer. This stunning stone is also a confidence booster and makes a great ring for making a commitment to yourself.

## AMAZONITE

Resembling the light green color of its namesake river, the Amazon, this potash feldspar, or microcline, is found in Russia, North America, and, naturally, Brazil. Green stones are frequently associated with the nervous system, and so is amazonite. This mentally stimulating crystal has the marvelous property of making the wearer more intuitive, smarter, or at least more clever; it provides focus. Amazonite should be held to your forehead to open your third eye for greater psychic ability. This is a stone for artists and is especially helpful for men.

## AMBER

The color amber is named after the stone, indicating how long people have been using this gem. A fossilized resin, amber comes from the sap of trees dating back millions of years. It frequently contains other fossils—insects, plant fragments, and rocks. Amber is prized for its honey gold color, but Baltic amber has a green color. Amber has been held in high regard as a power and protection talisman for thousands of years and has been used just as long as a healing stone, said to draw out disease, particularly afflictions of the thyroid, inner ear, spleen, brain, and lungs. You should clean amber after you use it because it draws in energy, which could include bad or negative energy from the body or the environment. Due to its organic origins, amber is an earth stone. It is so grounding and centering that you should not wear it all the time.

## AMETHYST

Amethyst is a purple quartz found most commonly in Brazil, Canada, and East Africa. The color can range from light violet to deep purple or can be nearly colorless. Amethyst has been prized for jewelry for hundreds of years, and before a huge cache was discovered in South America, it was valued as a precious gemstone. It is now classified as semiprecious.

It is one of the stones most esteemed by healers. The legendary American psychic Edgar Cayce recommended it for control and temperance. Amethyst is believed to aid in the production of hormones and regulate the circulatory, immune, and metabolic systems. Amethyst is treasured for its centering and calming properties and seems to connect directly to the mind, fighting emotional swings and depression. Aquarians and Pisceans can count it as their birthstone, and this might be a very good thing because the Fishes frequently struggle with substance-abuse issues, and amethyst can conquer drinking and other sensory indulgences, such as out-of-control sexuality. Amethyst also helps with mental focus, intuition, meditation, and memory.

In the early Renaissance, amethyst was held to have the power to prevent evil, at least evil thoughts, and to offer protection in time of war. This lovely purple gem continues to reign as one of the most popular of all stones. Little wonder, since it is such an aid to our physical and emotional health.

## ANDALUSITE

Sometimes referred to as the poor-man's alexandrite, andalusite is richly colored and changes in various light from a green to a red. It is playing a trick on the eye, however, because both colors are there at all times. This *pleochroic* quality means that the stone shows different colors when viewed from different directions. Tanzanite and alexandrite exhibit this same trait. Gemologists strive to reduce this feature, as it affects the quality and price of the stone, making it less valuable, but I personally love the different colors in the facets of a pleochroic gem. This stone, very popular in men's jewelry, was first found in Spain in the province of Andalusia. If you want people to see you in a different light, wear andalusite. This gem is particularly helpful if you're going for a promotion at work!

## APATITE

Here is a stone about which little is known. Apatite gets its name from the Greek word *apat?*, meaning "deceit," which is not so much a denigration of the stone itself but an expression that it comes in a vast array of green, yellow, violet, white, and brown colors that can easily confuse it with other like-colored crystals. Adding to the confusion is its varying opacity, from completely clear to milky. This stone is common to the Americas, Norway, southern India, and Russia.

Beneficial for hand-eye coordination and motor skills, apatite works best if you wear it in earrings or a thumb ring. If you are learning a new computer program or taking a painting or piano class, wear apatite to pick up the skills quickly.

## AQUAMARINE

Beloved for its crystal-clear blue color, this gem is a worldwide favorite. It is a form of beryl, as is emerald. Found in the Americas, Brazil, India, and Russia, aquamarine less frequently occurs in topaz-like yellow gold. Once upon a time, spectacles were made from aquamarine, but now it is cherished for the harmony it can bring. This stone is of particular use to psychics for filtering information and sharpening the sixth sense.

Once used by sailors as a guard against drowning, it is an aid for the throat and communication, even helping to express what is most difficult. This beautiful blue gem is the birthstone for those born in March, thus most Pisceans and a few early Aries. Aquamarine will help you become more intuitive *and* bring balance into your life.

## AVENTURINE

Associated with the eyes, this crystal is most commonly found in green, but it also appears in blue, red, and brown. Aventurine comes from Russia, India, Nepal, and Brazil and was at one time believed by Tibetans to be able to overcome myopia, both literally and figuratively. In Tibet, aventurine was also thought to have the ability to open the third eye and to release imagination and perception.

Considered to be beneficial to the thymus and the nervous system, aventurine is one of those rare general healers that can offer wellness to any part of the body upon which it is laid. As a general healing stone, it can also be used in tandem with other stones, such as rose quartz and malachite. Combined with rose quartz, aventurine can help open your heart and soul to love and compassion. Used in combination with malachite, the benefits are clarity and raised consciousness. Highly recommended and an excellent boon for young children, aventurine is a wonder stone for the well-being of the whole family.

## BERYL

Beryl, a blue, green, white, red, or yellow prismatic stone, comes from India, Brazil, the Czech Republic, Norway, France, Russia, and North America. The aforementioned aquamarine is a beryl, as is the precious emerald. These two members of the beryl family are much better known than beryl itself, but it is one of the most important gem minerals. Beryl is colorless in its pure form, called goshenite, but gains the lovely colorations through impurities. So, when one is talking about emerald, it is simply green beryl; aquamarine is blue beryl. Pink beryl is morganite, and yellow-green beryl is heliodor. To confuse the issue (or perhaps not), red beryl is referred to as red beryl, and golden beryl is called exactly that.

Beryl has a most unusual and important healing asset—it prevents people from doing the unnecessary. Further, it helps the wearers focus and remove distractions, and therefore become calmer and more positive. Beryl also strengthens the liver, kidneys, and intestines, as well as the pulmonary and circulatory systems. It is especially effective for the throat, and pulverized beryl can be mixed into an elixir specifically for this reason. Some crystal healers use beryl along with lapis lazuli as a sedative for nervous conditions. If you get overwhelmed at work or have a huge task ahead of you, efficiency-enhancing beryl will get you through it.

## BLOODSTONE

Known as the martyr's gem, bloodstone is actually green jasper with iron oxide impurities that result in brilliant red spots that rather resemble drops of blood in the pool of green. A traditional March birthstone, bloodstone was revered by the ancients, who saw it as a symbol of the setting sun casting its fiery red over the green ocean. It was once believed that this stone caused water to become red, which in turn made the sun red, giving it the power to affect the weather.

An ancient name for this variegated chalcedony quartz is "heliotrope." The gem is currently mined in Australia, North America, and India. It stands to reason that bloodstone would be connected with the blood and the circulatory system. It is also used to detoxify the blood, liver, kidneys, and spleen. A belief stemming from ancient times is that bloodstone can give great courage and help avoid harmful situations. In India, bloodstone is ground up and taken in an elixir as an aphrodisiac. All in all, bloodstone enriches the blood, calms the mind, and increases the consciousness of the wearer. Bloodstone is a great gem for you if you have a sedentary and detail-oriented job.

# CALCITE

Calcite, or limestone, is one of the more plentiful stones, coming in a range of colors from black to white, with every shade in between. Approximately 4 percent of Earth's surface is made up of calcite. Calcite gets its name from *chalix,* the Greek word for lime. Marble is limestone formed from heat and pressure, and calcite is the cement in many sandstones and shales. Calcite is the basis for many formations found in caves, such as cave veils, cave pearls, stalactites, and stalagmites. Environmentalists are heartened by this because this oceanic biological activity can act as a carbon-dioxide filter and help stem the greenhouse effect in the atmosphere.

The crystals in calcite can take on a thousand different shapes by combining the forms of rhombohedrons, scalahedrons, prisms, and pinacoids, to name but a few. More than 300 forms have been noted in calcite, and the symmetry is nearly unmatched, with many twins.

Calcite is all over the world, but certain conditions have made for very special specimens. In Cornwall, England; Pugh Quarry, Ohio; and Elmwood, Tennessee, are beautifully clear, amber-orange pyramid shapes called dogtooth spar. Mexican onyx, banded with orange, red, tan, brown, yellow, and white and having an appealing marble-like smoothness, is a very common type of calcite used in carvings sold in gift shops around the globe.

Calcite is helpful to bones and joints and is a memory booster. In addition to aiding in retaining information, calcite is a calming agent that can bring clarity to decision-making processes. Green calcite is a terrific support to people in transition, bringing about positive energy in place of the negative. The yellow and gold calcites are quite useful for meditation due to their association with the sun and with light, the sign of the spiritual path and higher knowledge. It is said that these sunny calcites can even help with astral projection. Calcite is a healing stone and is highly recommended for physicians, nurses, and healers to keep at their offices.

## CARNELIAN

If you have lost your lust for life and fallen into a pattern of old habits and uncreative day-to-day drudgery, this is the stone for you. Carnelian, also referred to in bygone days as carbuncle, is a type of quartz from the chalcedony gem family. Among the more abundantly available stones, it is found in Peru, Iceland, Romania, Britain, India, Pakistan, and the Czech Republic. Carnelian is a clear stone and is most commonly thought of as red, thus the name, but also comes in orange and occasionally very dark brown. It is found in pebble form and is translucent.

Carnelian has a long history and was used to cleanse other stones. It is an earth stone and acts as an anchor to the earth. Carnelian is thought to eliminate fear of death and is grounding and clarifying. In olden days, it was used as a sort of backward mirror to recall historical events. It is a lucky stone for people pursuing business ventures and for women hoping to have children. Carnelian is linked with the lower chakras and can heal holes in the etheric body and give support for letting go of anger, old resentments, and emotions that no longer serve a positive purpose. Orange carnelian is especially beloved for its ability to promote energy and vitality—to warm the emotions.

Part of the tradition around carnelian is that if worn at your throat it overcomes timidity and lends the power of great and eloquent speech. Like some other red stones, carnelian also gives you courage. In addition, wearing carnelian can offer you a sense of comfort with your environment and create the proper atmosphere for meditation and total clarity of mind and thought.

Carnelian as a pendant or belt gives you control of your thoughts and understanding of others.

## CELESTITE

Celestite takes its name from the heavenly blue color for which it is favored, though its range of hues includes shades of white and yellow. Celestite, mined for its salts and the strontium it contains, has another connection to the sky in that it is used in fireworks, where it flames a fiery crimson. Celestite has occurred notably in the Great Lakes Region of North America as well as in Sicily, Germany, and Madagascar. It is sometimes mistaken for its look-alike, barite, but a flame test will tell the truth. If the flame is a pale green, the mineral is barite, but if it is red, it is most certainly celestite.

Celestite, which resonates with all the chakras, is most powerful. A geode of celestite crystal is believed to be filled with angel energy and brings the highest consciousness. It is a great balancing stone, creating attunement with high intellect and evening out male and female energies within any person.

Celestite is the stone to keep with you before any speaking engagements or writing that you need to do and do well. It aids the flow of thoughts and words. Most interestingly of all, it is a "listening stone." Hold a piece of celestite and listen carefully to the voice within; the wisdom from this stone will reveal your deepest intuition and lead you to the right action. Meditation is greatly assisted by this crystal, as it is believed to hold the wisdom of the archangels. In meditation, you can ask celestite for any knowledge you need and it will be made known to you, whether it is a memory of a past life, a vision, or an out-of-body experience. Celestite is also a dream stone to keep by your bed for insight into the meaning of your night visions.

### STONES, SIGNS, AND NUMBERS

As we know, crystals and gems have specific relationships with different astrological signs, many of which were determined by the Chaldeans of long ago. All you have to remember is that the stone's optimum effect will take place if it is related to the correlating astrological sign. For example, Cancers can wear pearls to express and protect their sensitive inner natures. The effect will be even greater when the Sun is in Cancer, and greatest of all when the Moon is in Cancer, too. Scorpios will be even more powerful than usual when sporting rubies during their birth month, and so on.

By the same token, gems and crystals vibrate to different numbers. This all has to do with energy. Each letter of the alphabet is associated with a number, as indicated by this chart:

| 1 | 2 | 3 | 4 | 5 | 6 | 7 | 8 | 9 |
|---|---|---|---|---|---|---|---|---|
| a | b | c | d | e | f | g | h | i |
| j | k | l | m | n | o | p | q | r |
| s | t | u | v | w | x | y | z |   |

So, my name is Brenda, which adds up to 26, which adds up to 8 (2 + 6). Thus, I should work with and try wearing jet, the stone corresponding to the number 8. And you know what? I have never had jet, and I believe I have been missing out. I must remedy that at once!

| Number 1 | Stone or Metal | Corresponding Sign(s) |
|---|---|---|
|  | Aquamarine | Aries, Gemini, Pisces |
|  | Beryl | Leo |
|  | Copper | Taurus, Sagittarius |
|  | Obsidian | Sagittarius |
|  | Turquoise | Scorpio, Sagittarius, Pisces |

| Number 2 | Stone or Metal | Corresponding Sign(s) |
|---|---|---|
| | Garnet | Leo, Virgo, Capricorn, Aquarius |
| | Sapphire | Virgo, Libra, Sagittarius |
| | Tourmaline | Libra |

| Number 3 | Stone or Metal | Corresponding Sign(s) |
|---|---|---|
| | Amber | Leo, Aquarius |
| | Amethyst | Virgo, Capricorn, Aquarius, Pisces |
| | Aventurine | Aries |
| | Herkimer diamond | Sagittarius |
| | Lapis lazuli | Sagittarius |
| | Ruby | Cancer, Leo, Scorpio, Sagittarius |

| Number 4 | Stone or Metal | Corresponding Sign(s) |
|---|---|---|
| | Bloodstone | Aries, Libra, Pisces |
| | Emerald | Aries, Taurus, Gemini |
| | Moonstone | Cancer, Libra, Scorpio |
| | Quartz | All |
| | Sodalite | Sagittarius |
| | Tiger's-eye | Capricorn |

| Number 5 | Stone or Metal | Corresponding Sign(s) |
|---|---|---|
| | Amazonite | Virgo |
| | Carnelian | Taurus, Cancer, Leo |
| | Peridot | Leo, Virgo, Scorpio, Sagittarius |

| Number 6 | Stone or Metal | Corresponding Sign(s) |
|---|---|---|
| | Apache tear | Aries |
| | Bloodstone | Aries, Libra, Pisces |
| | Carnelian | Taurus, Cancer, Leo |

| 6 (cont.) | Stone or Metal | Corresponding Sign(s) |
|---|---|---|
| | Cat's-eye | Aries, Taurus, Capricorn |
| | Citrine | Aries, Leo, Libra |
| | Moldavite | Scorpio |
| | Onyx | Leo |
| | Peridot | Leo, Virgo, Scorpio, Sagittarius |

| Number 7 | Stone or Metal | Corresponding Sign(s) |
|---|---|---|
| | Agate | Gemini |
| | Pearl | Gemini, Cancer |
| | Peridot | Leo, Virgo, Scorpio, Sagittarius |
| | Rose quartz | Taurus, Libra |

| Number 8 | Stone or Metal | Corresponding Sign(s) |
|---|---|---|
| | Chrysolite | Taurus |
| | Jet | Capricorn |
| | Opal | Cancer, Libra, Scorpio |

| Number 9 | Stone or Metal | Corresponding Sign(s) |
|---|---|---|
| | Hematite | Aries, Aquarius |
| | Malachite | Scorpio, Capricorn |

## Other

Chrysolite is both 8 and the master number 55 and is under Taurus rulership.
(The *master number* represents a high potential for growth and understanding.)

Diamond is the master number 33 and is ruled by Aries, Taurus, and Leo.

Fluorite vibrates to every number and corresponds to Capricorn and Pisces.

Jade vibrates to the master number 11 and relates to Aries, Taurus, Gemini, and Libra.

# CHALCEDONY

This member of the quartz family is also a gem family in and of itself, including cat's-eye, tiger's-eye, jasper, onyx, agate, and carnelian. It is a fine-grained and multihued type of silica mineral quartz with a waxy patina. Chalcedony most commonly occurs in a white, gray, yellow, brown, or light tan form known as chert. It is the result of silica's replacing the original organic material—sea sponges, fish, plants, or wood from trees. Some spectacular chert specimens are the petrified trees in Arizona's Petrified Forest National Park; their brilliant reds and greens are due to the traces of iron contained within, giving them an otherworldly effect.

As chalcedony is actually a stone from some of Earth's earliest living things, it has been with us since man's earliest days and has been used in tools and as adornment. It is still actively produced in South America, primarily in Uruguay and Brazil, as well as in the southwest part of Africa. Known as the stone of brotherhood, chalcedony was sacred to Native Americans and was a powerful stone used to unite tribes in holy ceremonies. It is a stone of stability, kindness, endurance, and balance and is said to create peace. Chalcedony engenders a desire for introspection and can help overcome low self-esteem and bring about enthusiasm for a new lease on life. This star-powered crystal can also prevent loss of mental faculties as you age. Keep your memory intact with chalcedony!

This crystal is best if you wear it in a ring, a necklace, or a belt. It is a cleansing stone and can even assist you with healing your skin. Chalcedony is most unusual in that it doesn't have to be cleansed after each use. It absorbs negative energy and is a protector; exposure to ultraviolet light will increase these cleansing powers. An old wives' tale (literally) is that chalcedony promotes both lactation and the maternal instinct and is, therefore, a mother's stone. The ancient Egyptians recorded many medicinal formulas made up of powdered chalcedony. Don't drink it, however; wear it to stay smart and soothe your soul and your skin.

## CHRYSOBERYL

This underknown gem has two siblings, alexandrite and cat's-eye, that have stolen all the attention away from the lovely but less showy green, yellow, and brown transparent type of chrysoberyl. The stone occurs in Canada, Norway, Australia, Ghana, Burma, the Ural Mountains in Russia, and the other gem havens of Sri Lanka and Brazil. It appears in rare instances as a cyclic crystal that looks to be hexagonal but is a triplet of three twins called a trilling.

Cousin cat's-eye, also called cymophane, occurs in colorations ranging from honey gold to bright green. It usually comes in a domed cabochon shape. If intense light is shone in a cat's-eye, one side will look milky and the other will remain golden; this is known as the milk-and-honey effect. The *eye effect* is the result of infinitesimal needle-like inclusions that refract light, creating a line of light that runs through the center. A handful of other stones, scapolite, spinel, quartz, tourmaline, and corundum, have a similar appearance as a result of these inclusions, but only chrysoberyl can be called just cat's-eye; the others require the stone name in front of cat's-eye. Cat's-eye has been used to manifest destiny and direct fortune for centuries and makes an excellent talisman.

Healers prize chrysoberyl because it can double the power of other stones and reveal the causes of illness. It can assist with lowering high cholesterol and the hormonal surges of adrenaline. Chrysoberyl is a crystal used for compassion, forgiveness, and emotional release and has been called the stone of new beginnings. This is one of the few crystals that can enable one to see both sides of an issue and get over blocks and stubbornness. If you are harboring a grudge against a coworker or loved one, chrysoberyl will cut right through the old anger and help you to move on.

## CHRYSOCOLLA

A green or blue opaque stone, chrysocolla is almost never heard of outside of gem circles. Many people think it is a symbol of Earth due to its blue-and-green planet-like patterning. It is a stone with a gentle energy, unlike many other stones that have intense energy, such as some quartzes, lapis, malachite, and obsidian. It occurs in Zaire, Russia, North America, and Chile.

Tranquil chrysocolla is a heart stone that affects the heart chakra, enabling the gentle release of emotions, guilt, and fear. It is a truth stone. It can ease the pain and discomfort of arthritis and bone or skeletal issues. Ulcers, stomach pain, and intestinal problems are greatly alleviated with this healer.

The stone is associated with Gaia—our Earth Mother—and also Kwan Yin, the benevolent bringer of compassion. Chrysocolla evokes the qualities of these goddesses: nurturing, forgiveness, and tolerance. It is viewed as a lunar stone, perfect for new-moon meditations and meditations on global issues such as the environment and world peace. By merely holding this placid piece of earth in your hand, you can help send healing energy out to the planet at large.

Egyptians favored chrysocolla as an amulet for protection. This earthy stone can give confidence to the shy and empower them to speak the truth. Thus, chrysocolla would make a wonderful accessory to wear as a choker or near the throat when giving any kind of public speech. This beautifully oceanic rock can also give the wearer a better ability for listening, the all-important other component to communication. It amplifies sensitivity to aid in understanding what is spoken as well as unspoken. This generous crystal was traditionally used by musicians for its ability to ease expression and give greater beauty to the singing voice.

Chrysocolla also increases the capacity for love, one of the sweetest and most beneficial qualities any stone can offer. But my favorite feature of chrysocolla is that it tells you when to be silent and when to speak. It doesn't get better than that!

## CHRYSOLITE

This stone, also known as olivine or as peridot, its popular name, is commonly found among the crystal of meteorites, with a glassy luster and a great degree of hardness coming from the mountainous regions of Russia, North America, and Italy. A common mistake people make with the green or yellow versions of this stone is to confuse them with topaz. Chrysolite has long-held associations with the sun and solar energies as well as the month of August. For centuries it has been used to drive away evil spirits and madness. It is a stone of hope, having the capacity to free the self from sorrow and despair. If you are going through an especially difficult time, wear chrysolite until you have gotten past the pain.

This cheerful crystal gives inspiration. Chrysolite is a creativity crystal. It frees the imagination and counteracts negativity. For people who feel hampered by the rules of society and unable to truly express themselves and their inner beings, this stone is a great boost to personal freedom. Depressives can also find solace here. Chrysolite provides ease to those who feel careworn and overburdened. This uplifting stone also lends better psychic insight and receptivity, a great aid to meditation.

Chrysolite is a cleanser believed to assist the appendix and help with detoxifying the intestinal tract. Detox your body *and* mind with cheery chrysolite.

# CHRYSOPRASE

This apple green stone is a quartz—or more specifically, a form of chalcedony—mined in Brazil, Australia, North America, and Russia. The lovely, dazzling green is derived from the nickel content in its chemical makeup. The bright green makes chrysoprase perfect for abundance and prosperity. Put this in your money corner.

The color and clarity give chrysoprase its power to impart good cheer, good luck, and increased perception. Healthwise, it assists the eyes and the third eye. It gives rise to issues simmering in the unconscious and makes these concealed concerns easier to deal with once they have surfaced. It can also draw forth talents that have lain dormant. Chrysoprase is like a battery; it stores energy. For many centuries, this green crystal was used as medicine for the mentally ill. It dispels anxiety by reducing fear and also opening the mind to new patterns. Chrysoprase can be a source of calm for you during change.

The stone is especially useful for scholars. The brilliance booster is an agent of calm yet also a stimulator of intellectual curiosity, two seemingly incompatible traits. I love that it reduces egotism and increases creativity, but others no doubt prize this green crystal for the sexual protection it offers—increased fertility and a guard against contact-transmitted diseases. Chrysoprase will also keep you from getting gout and from going crazy!

This is a crystal to keep in a dream bag beneath your pillow to help with relaxation, promote restful sleep, and gain new insights. Beneficial for the heart chakra, this money-colored stone will create an atmosphere of encouragement, a wonderful gift to yourself.

## CORAL

Coral is another stone formed from organic material. In this case, it is the skeletons of many sea creatures. Coral can be found all around the world in our oceans. Ancient cultures revered coral for its medical benefits and its beauty. The ancients attributed much religious significance to coral as well. Coral comes in a nearly infinite number of shapes, and the colors range almost as widely—from white to black. The different colors of coral have different properties:

+ pink is comforting;
+ red is invigorating;
+ gray brings accord;
+ black absorbs energy;
+ white brings constancy.

Coral abets the bones and the blood and is a cleanser, good for inner organs and mental processes. Edgar Cayce used it to pacify and soothe. Since coral is made up of many generations of organisms, it is a gateway to the past. Because it was so readily available—by washing up on shore and being easily harvested from the seas—ancient man believed sailors could calm the waters with it. It was commonly worn as an amulet and pendant, with the most powerful coral having been freshly taken from the ocean unbroken. The ancients believed the living being remained inside the coral until it was broken, giving it enormous power. Moonlight is supposed to intensify the healing power of coral. Use the color guidelines above to help you choose the coral you need at any given time. You should provide yourself with an entire wardrobe of corals in all shades. Wear a red coral necklace to rid yourself of a chest cold; wear gray if you are squabbling with your mate. Wear white if you need more "Zen" in your world.

## CUPRITE

Here is a mineral crystal formed from copper ore. Cuprite can have needle-like crystals of a brilliant red, a true red, inside a nearly black crystal. Cuprite has a spectacular sparkle. It is found most frequently in France, Russia, North America, Germany, Britain, and Australia. In the same way that copper has wonderful health benefits, so does cuprite, helping with concerns in the heart, blood, skin, muscles, and bones. Cuprite stimulates the lower chakra. It is a handy stone to take along on air flights, as it can treat altitude sickness. It also furthers the functions of the bladder and kidneys.

Cuprite has another feature not found in other stones—it can help one deal with male authority figures. This may come, in part, from cuprite's revelatory power to connect with your past lives. If you have father issues you need to overcome, I strongly suggest this stone. The unusual magic it offers is also good for dealing with male coworkers and bosses.

## DANBURITE

Danburite is gaining attention after being relatively unknown. Named for the city of Danbury, Connecticut, where it was first found, danburite is a typically white or clear vitreous crystal that can also come in shades of pink, brown, or yellow. Some of the finest specimens come from Japan, and some of the largest from Siberia, but danburite is also found in Bolivia, the Czech Republic, Switzerland, and Mexico. Danburite is also notable for its diamond-shaped cross section. Anyone who likes utterly transparent crystal clusters will favor this stone, which is an activator of the chakras, particularly the third eye and the crown. This crystal is finding great acceptance for its ability to blend your heart and soul energies. Place danburite on your heart and on your forehead to fully receive the positive effects.

Healthwise, danburite can help underweight people gain muscle and vigor. It also detoxifies the liver and gallbladder and assists with motor function. Although it is a newer citizen of the crystal world, danburite is becoming known for its invaluable attributes in increasing intelligence and easing unfamiliar situations. It can overcome stubbornness and bring patience and peace. Get yourself some danburite if you are in a new job, a new city, or a new relationship. This stone will help you surf the waters of change with ease!

## Throwing Stones

Give your tarot cards a rest and create a one-of-a-kind divination tool, a bag of crystals you can do readings with. It is very easy to do. I have stones that I tumbled as a child and others I have picked up on travels. Even yesterday, I grabbed some garnets, agates, and tiny citrines at the Psychic Eye on Fell and Gough Streets in San Francisco to add to my bag of goodies. I have a favorite blue velvet bag, and when the need arises, I turn to crystal visions for my enlightenment. If you are like me, you *cannot* afford diamonds in your bag of tricks, so substitute them with clear quartz; for emeralds, switch to peridots. Garnets substitute nicely for rubies. I was happy to note that the Psychic Eye had rough-ruby and rough-emerald pieces at $3 each, so the real deal is more available all the time. It is as easy as one, two, three: 1) shake the bag well, 2) ask a question, and 3) remove the first three stones you touch and then interpret from the following guide:

- **Agate:** Business success and notoriety are near.
- **Amethyst:** Change is coming.
- **Aventurine:** New horizons and positive growth are ahead.
- **Black agate:** Monetary gain is certain.

- ◆ **Blue lace agate:** There's a need for spiritual and physical healing.
- ◆ **Citrine:** The universe offers enlightenment.
- ◆ **Diamond:** Stability is sure.
- ◆ **Emerald:** Look for lushness.
- ◆ **Hematite:** Examine new prospects.
- ◆ **Jade:** Life is everlasting.
- ◆ **Lapis lazuli:** Harness heavenly fortune.
- ◆ **Quartz:** Receive clarity where there was none.
- ◆ **Red agate:** Expect long life and health.
- ◆ **Red jasper:** Notice the need for grounding.
- ◆ **Rose quartz:** Love is in your life.
- ◆ **Ruby:** Dare for deep passion and personal power.
- ◆ **Sapphire:** Time for truth.
- ◆ **Snowflake obsidian:** Your troubles are at an end.
- ◆ **Snow quartz:** Make major changes.
- ◆ **Tiger's-eye:** The situation is not as it appears.

## DENDRITE

In manganese-ore sources, treelike or fern-shaped mineral growths sometimes occur. These are called dendrites. This is the same pattern of growth that happens in ice crystals when the liquid crystal molecules diffuse in the air before attaching to the solid crystal surface. Crystal dendrites have the ability to open and cleanse all the chakras. Unique and interesting-looking, dendrite is great to have around when you are resting and rejuvenating.

## DIAMOND

Now we come to the mighty diamond, a gemstone revered the world over and the lucky birthstone of the April-born. This is generally considered to be the highest and purest expression of gems. The clarity of diamonds and their ability to refract light are peerless. Composed of pure carbon, diamonds are formed after thousands of years of great pressure and heat at great depth below the earth's crust in iron-magnesium magma. Diamonds were first brought to the earth's surface by volcanic flows and are now mined at great cost in Siberia, Australia, South Africa, and Arkansas. In Canada and California, glaciers have pushed diamonds near the surface, creating some great episodes in history.

When exposed to radiation, diamonds will phosphoresce and are generally considered to be the hardest natural substance. Poor-grade, or *bort,* diamonds are often used for industrial purposes, but gem cutters in India have become expert at finding ways to salvage these lower-quality diamonds for use in jewelry.

Diamonds are terrific healing stones; perhaps no other crystal can focus energy so purely and intensely. The lore surrounding the healing qualities of diamonds is vast, but most healers agree that the unique blue light of this gem is a help to the eye condition glaucoma. Diamonds are also thought to be a boon to male genitalia, bringing some interesting jewelry options to mind. Diamonds are superb in conjunction with other stones and will amplify the properties of any other gem. While this can be enormously helpful, it cuts both ways. If you are in a negative state of mind, diamonds will amplify that, as well.

Diamond has come to be a symbol of fidelity and is the traditional stone used in a ring for engagement, a pledge to be married and together forever. Since this gem is an aid to intuition, the ring itself will help the potential bride know if her betrothed is really "the one." Diamonds also imbue courage and can help one face anything.

## DIAMONDS ARE YOUR BRAIN'S BEST FRIEND

This most precious of stones reputedly does wonders for the brain if worn as earrings. Therefore, I deem diamond earrings as essential. Quick, tell your mate!

## DIOPTASE

Dioptase is a gorgeous gemstone that is nearly the color of emerald but lacks the hardness, thus lowering its marketplace value. It can be found in Peru, Chile, Russia, Iran, and some sites in Africa. The true value of dioptase lies in its ability to help anyone experiencing mental stress. It lends balance to male and female energies and acts as a stabilizer. As an energy stone, dioptase can activate and awaken every chakra, invigorating the mind, body, and spirit. If you want to be really different, wear dioptase, and you will fascinate admirers with this beautiful stone and find peace of mind in the process.

## RECESSION-PROOF ROCK

When the economy starts to slide, secure your job with petrified wood. This security stone will be your bulwark when the marketplace sands begin to shift. As an added bonus, it can make you physically stronger. Keep it on your desk and touch it when you feel worried and you will immediately feel calmer and more grounded.

## Tips 'n' Tricks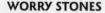

### WORRY STONES

Pinkish red stones offer enormous psychological support. Turn to such rose stones—rhodochrosite, rhodonite, and rhyolite—during times of trouble and they will come to your emotional rescue. Keep them in your pocket or purse or in a desk drawer so you can hold them in your hand when you feel scared. Harmony will abound.

### EMERALD

This fantastical green gem has been doted on for 4,000 years. The word "emerald" comes from the Greek word *smaragdos,* meaning "green stone." While diamonds have many, many fans, emeralds have their enthusiasts, as well. I am a huge fan of emeralds and had one hand-made by a South African goldsmith to pair with the diamonds in the setting for my engagement ring.

As mentioned previously, emerald is also known as green beryl. It is the most valuable of all the beryls—a precious gem, indeed. Beryl is usually colorless but becomes green when traces of chromium appear in its makeup. This occurs rarely, which is why emeralds are so costly.

Gems are, of course, judged for their brilliance, clarity, weight, and proportion. Emeralds have to be cut in a certain way—the very popular octagonal shape that has come to be called the emerald cut—because they are considered to be sensitive stones. The less transparent or very included stones are often mounted as dome-shaped cabochons.

Lucky May-born folks have emerald, the gem of joy and positivity, as their special stone. The gem is a symbol of true love, fidelity, fertility, and birth. Emeralds create harmony, the lubricant of life, and also help the memory. They help people express themselves well, and they add to that power by promoting the telling of only the truth. Emeralds are wisdom stones that give the wearers the inspiration and intuition to share their wisdom with others and to shower love on the people in their lives. Health issues that are reputedly alleviated by emerald include diabetes, problems in the spine, back, and skeleton, and mental and emotional stress. The stone is heralded to be a balm for irritated eyes.

Emerald is also a heart stone, offering benefits on physical and emotional planes. I prefer emeralds above all other stones for engagement rings. This is your ultimate gem for happiness in a relationship. In fact, emerald has been called the stone of successful love and can engender utter felicity, total loyalty, and domestic bliss in a willing couple. The emerald is at its most powerful if worn as a pinkie- or ring-finger ornament or in a bracelet on the right wrist. But wearers, be warned! Do *not* wear emerald at all times or its superpositive force starts to reverse. A little emerald luck goes a long way.

## ENSTATITE

Enstatite is a fairly common mineral found in Russia, Japan, Germany, North America, and Ireland. It is found in metamorphic rock and occasionally some igneous sites, but the more exciting finds are from meteorites. Enstatite occurs in a couple of gemstone forms: one called bronzite and another called chrome-enstatite, a less-common green variety that contains traces of chromium, the same agent that causes the green color in emeralds.

Enstatite is used for the circulatory system and as a cleanser for organs such as the liver and kidneys. This stone is also a "mental cleanser," favored by students, teachers, physicians, and professionals who have to think on their feet, such as public speakers and attorneys. If you have work or a project that requires heavy concentration or is very taxing mentally, keep enstatite on hand.

## SPACE INVADERS

Do you have nosy neighbors or a nightmare roommate? Combat other people's cluelessness with crystals! If you have problems with the people next door, place jet at your door or bury it by the fence. If you have an intrusive housemate or guest, place jet on the mantle or bookshelves and wear jet jewelry to take back your personal space straightaway.

## FIRE AGATE

This interesting specimen has small, thin layers that allow light to fill them with what is known as fire. Really, the effect occurs due to the inclusions of very thin layers of iridescent limonite, which cause the light to refract in differing colors. Fire agate is formed when silica-laden water is heated and mixed with iron oxide, filling the cracks between rocks and then cooling into this interesting stone. Most often found in India, Iceland, Brazil, North America, and the Czech Republic, fire agate needs to be cut in just such a way to feature the layers; one wrong cut and the fire agate is ruined. The process of cutting fire agate is a reversal of Mother Nature's process.

Fire agate is favored for its iridescent appearance; some believe it is the physical manifestation of the spiritual flame, one of absolute perfection. Fire agate brings the wearer courage and the ability to fend off fear. The fire inside this agate provides a protective shield that actually sends fright back to its source. Fire agate causes a sense of calm and a greater connection to the planet. It is a very useful mind-clearing stone for meditation. Fire agate is wonderfully conducive to introspection, helping to bring deep-seated issues to the surface so they can be examined in the clear light of day. Orange stones are thought to be the most powerful for their high degree of stimulation and for their ability to reveal the hidden.

Fire agate brings out the best in you with this positive, cardinal energy; it propels you forward for advancement in both the spiritual sense and in the real world of work and success. Fire agate can be placed upon the meridians of the body in the same way an acupuncturist or acupressure healer lays on hands. In this way, any sensory blockage can be cleared away, and nervous and circulatory issues can be dealt with.

This is a healer's stone—the companion for doctors, shamans, dentists, and psychologists. It is also a cleansing agent of the stomach and glands and is great for the eyes, even said to improve night vision. And, as one might guess with fire, this agate is a sexuality stone. So, light the flame within with fearless agate. Make sure you're sporting this sexy gem when you are planning a big seduction!

## FLINT

Flint is probably not thought of as a crystal, let alone as a healing crystal, but it is a variety of quartz whose crystal structure is not visible to the eye. Flint most commonly occurs in the form of rounded nodules in a grayish black color. If it is found near chalk, it will have a white coating. Flint can also be red or brown in color, and it is found all over the world.

Early humans in the Stone Age cultures of the Pleistocene era appreciated the hardness of this practical crystal, and they used it to make crude tools and spearheads. More-modern men used flint to set off the gunpowder in flintlock guns. It is unfortunate that flint came to be so relied upon for weapons, as its energy can actually be very beneficial to the tissue of the human body. Flint gives an allover sense of well-being, not just in the body but also the mind. The special gift flint gives is a renewed sense of strength and gentle healing power to those suffering from degenerative diseases. Flint in your home will ground you and create a sense of safety and comfort.

## FLUORITE

Fluorite comes in every color of the rainbow and features a bonus—its fluorescent quality produces a special, rather eerie glow under ultraviolet light. Pure fluorite (simple fluorine and calcium) is colorless. Colored fluorite—in oceanic green, dark purple, buttery yellow, pale amethyst, or bright blue—results from traces of other elements.

Fluorite is dualistic in its opacity—it can be crystal-clear or translucent. Fluorite is rather like glass except it's brittle and soft, which keeps it out of the running as a precious gemstone, even though it is just as beautiful to look at and polishes to a brilliant, glossy surface. The yielding surface scratches easily, making it an unfortunate choice for a ring. Fluorite is best worn as an earring, close to the brain and neck and spine, areas where it offers enormous assistance and healing. Even as a pin or pendant, it must be handled very gingerly to avoid damage or scratches to the surface.

Fluorite is commonly found in China, Peru, Norway, Australia, Britain, and several areas of North America. The state of Illinois has massive fluorite deposits, which formed around 150 million years ago from the fluorinated (by Mother Nature herself!) water that was heated and rose to a high level during the Jurassic period, flowing all around limestone deposits from the earlier Mississippian period of 330 million years ago. This fluorine-rich brine hit the calcium-laden limestone, and the conditions were perfect for the crystallization of fluorite. Think about that for a moment. The crystal you hold in your hand may well have formed 100 million years ago. What vast energy must be contained inside!

I find it somewhat amusing that fluorine flowed in ancient river waters naturally, and now we have fluoride (a compound of fluorine) put into the drinking water of today to strengthen teeth and prevent tooth decay. There is a link, however, because fluorite is also beneficial to bones and teeth. The ancients used it to treat growths and cancers. Fluorite sparks the mentality and can bring on deeply meaningful epiphanies. In addition to being beneficial for arthritis, sports injuries, and skeletal issues, fluorite is a boon to sexuality, said to be Mother Nature's Viagra! Fluorite creates conditions wherein the gentle release of sexual anxiety and libido problems is possible. On your second honeymoon, take a chunk of fluorite crystal to the hotel—ooh la la!

## Tips 'n' Tricks

### A RAINBOW OF USES FOR FLUORITE

Violet- or amethyst-colored fluorite is especially good for the bones, including the marrow. It jogs the third eye and, best of all, imparts good old common sense! Green fluorite is favored for its ability to ground and center excessive physical and mental energy. Clear fluorite awakens the crown chakra and lets go of anything holding back spiritual development. Blue fluorite facilitates mental clarity, orderly thought, and the ability to be a master communicator. Yellow fluorite kindles the synapses and awakens memory. It will also make you smarter and boost your creativity a great deal.

Any fluorite reduces electromagnetic pollutants and cleanses the aura. Get a big chunk of fluorite at your favorite metaphysical five-and-dime and put it right beside your computer to decrease stress. Those long hours of staring at the screen will cease to sap your energy. Look at your fluorite at least once an hour to reduce eye and brain strain, too!

# GARNET

I love that the word "garnet" comes from *granatum,* referring to the color of a pomegranate seed—how mythic and romantic! (And much more appealing than the word coined by the Egyptians, "carbuncle.") Garnet has come to be considered a wine-colored stone, but in actuality, it can come in green, yellow, or brown. Garnets are found all over the world and make up a family of minerals:

+ **Almandite,** the most common of the garnets and probably the favorite, is dark red with a deep brown cast; its rich color is brought on by the content of iron and aluminum. It is often cut as a jewel.

+ **Andradite** is a combination of calcium and iron and varies in color from red to green to yellow to black. Green andradites are favored as gems.

+ **Grossular,** composed of calcium and aluminum, occurs most often in a white or clear color. In Sri Lanka, there is a topaz-like brown grossular that is of jewel quality, and in Siberia, there is one that's gooseberry green—thus the name "grossular," derived from the Latin word for this fruit.

+ **Pyrope** is the most precious garnet, with the clearest red color due to the magnesium content. The most valuable pyropes come from South Africa, in the "blue earth" where diamonds are found.

+ **Spessartine** is the rarest garnet, an aluminum-and-manganese gem with an appealing orange tint.

+ **Uvarovite** is not very common. This grassy green garnet is usually discovered in calcium-rich serpentine rock and has a unique crystalline structure.

Red garnets are love stones. These sexy stones can help those with a lethargic libido tune into their passion. Green garnets are the real healing stones. These crystals offer protection to the chakras. You should wear green garnets as earrings or in a necklace to get the most benefit from the inner and outer healing power.

Garnets are conductors of past-life memories and are memory sharpeners in the here and now. They offer the welcome advantage of increasing patience. Garnets also promote compassion and awareness of the world and the self. They help a person to let go, especially of self-loathing.

## HEMATITE

Hematite takes its otherworldly metallic sheen from the iron oxide of which it is made. Even way back in the "Stone Age," when I had my rock tumbler, I could quite easily come up with a silvery pebble after tumbling and polishing hematite. Occasionally, hematite has a reddish color or red speckles on the surface. This may be why hematite is named thusly; the root of the word, *haima,* is the Greek word for blood. Hematite has long been associated with blood, blood rituals, and medicine for treating nosebleeds, menstruation, heart disease, anemia, kidney disease, hemophilia, birth, surgery, insomnia, lung problems, and fever. Native Americans use hematite in dentistry and to treat wounds and substance abuse. Ancient Egyptians ground hematite up and put it in medicines and unguents. Egyptians loved this glistening rock, and every person could have one (which wasn't the case with emeralds). They frequently wore hematite as an amulet, believing it could render the wearer invincible.

Hematite is most frequently found in North America, Sweden, Britain, Switzerland, Italy, and Brazil. Hematite is almost like the "Magic Metals" previously discussed (see chapter two) because it contains high levels of iron, driving its blood-cleaning capabilities. It is also a protective rock and fortifies tissue regeneration. Hematite shores up self-image and self-belief. It also transforms negative energy into positive. Hematite is considered to be yang, a more male energy. My preferred aspect of this shiny wonder is that it assists with both legal problems and astral projection. Hematite is a creativity crystal and a marvelous mental enhancer, increasing the ability to think with logic, to focus, to concentrate, and to remember more clearly and completely. Hematite draws anxiety out of the body and creates calm. In addition to all of these aspects that project outward, hematite contributes to inner work: self-knowledge, deeper consciousness, and wisdom. Like the iron in the earth from which it is formed, hematite grounds. If you feel spacey or disconnected, you should wear hematite.

You now know that hematite can be found fairly commonly in North America and parts of South America, but you may not be aware that it can be found in plenitude on Mars! Yes, Mars has a bad case of "rust" due to the gray hematite in a massive patch on the surface near the Martian equator, proving that Mars had water or at least water vapor at some point. This has led to tantalizing theories from scientists about possible hot springs that were once active on our red neighbor planet. I discovered this while cruising the NASA Web site. How do they know it was hematite? Through an infrared-imaging system known as THEMIS (Thermal Emission Imaging System). I also discovered a quote by Victoria Hamilton, a planetary geologist at Arizona State University, explaining that "all materials vibrate at the atomic scale . . . each mineral has a unique infrared spectrum that identifies it as surely as the fingerprints of a human being." Fascinating!

## Tips 'n' Tricks

### SALESPERSON'S STONE

If you are in sales and marketing, you simply must get some carnelian jewelry to wear and some carnelian crystals to put on your desk to turn it into a manifestation station! I know of one woman who surrounded herself with this lively agate and she doubled her dollars. This rock will help *you* to rock in your job and soar up the corporate ladder!

### HAWK'S-EYE

Hawk's-eye is an abundance stone. It can look very much like its namesake, the eye of the powerful bird. This underknown crystal is a darker version of tiger's-eye. It occurs in South Africa, North America, India, and Australia and is banded like its brother stone. Hawk's-eye has strong earth energy. It has the rare ability to calm and energize at the same time. While tiger's-eye is about taking in the long view, hawk's-eye is about taking the aerial vantage point, a detached viewpoint.

Hawk's-eye has a blue-green glint, while tiger's-eye is yellow gold. Both offer flashes of insight from different perspectives. In many cultures, hawks are the messengers of the gods. In the same way, you can hold this stone to your third eye or in the palm of your hand and ask for deep wisdom. Wait and listen, and the answer will come to you. I love this stone because it attracts not only wealth and material objects but also people who are good for you and bring advantageous connections. Hawk's-eye is your solace when you are in real trouble and can't see your way out. As a healer, it is good for the circulatory system, the legs, the bowels, and the eyes, of course. Photographers, scientists, airline pilots, and anyone whose vision is essential to their success would do well to wear hawk's-eye at work.

## DIAMOND DREAMS

If you place a Herkimer diamond beneath your pillow, you will have incredibly vivid dreams, which you should keep track of in a dream journal and discuss or study in dream work. If the power of these dreams is overwhelming, you can make it more manageable by placing an amethyst beside the Herkimer diamond, which will moderate the intensity of the dreams.

Herkimer diamonds are power stones, bringing great vitality and exuberance into your life. They can redirect stress away from you with their absorptive abilities. Placing these rocks in your bedroom will cause stress to melt away and help you relax and feel safe.

Lastly, if you live anywhere near a nuclear facility of any kind, whether it is a power station or medical hospital that performs radiation, this stone will absorb the radiation and help protect you and your loved ones. Herkimer diamonds retain the memory imprint of what they have born witness to in their environment and reflect back to us a gentle understanding of what they have seen. I have a Herkimer diamond pendant that evokes many compliments. I was attracted to it at the International New Age Trade Show in Denver in 1999 and couldn't stop thinking about it. Later, when I was diagnosed with breast cancer, to the amazement of all my friends and family, I didn't need radiation or chemotherapy, and I think I know why!

## HERKIMER DIAMOND

First off, this is not a diamond. It is a clear quartz first discovered in Herkimer, New York. It was exclusively mined there until recently, when it was uncovered in Oaxaca, Mexico. The reason it is nicknamed diamond is because of its brilliance, sparkle, and diamond shape. It also has a lovely rainbow-like effect at its center—optimism at the very core.

This crystal releases energy blockage and is helpful to the chakras. Herkimer diamond is a stone of attunement. It is most effective if placed upon each chakra area in need of therapy. For example, if you are having difficulty speaking about something that troubles you, place a Herkimer diamond on your throat. If you are brokenhearted, place it on the heart chakra. Some crystal healers believe the greatest power of the Herkimer is the prevention of illness.

My penchant for this stone lies in its ability to bring tremendously meaningful, prophetic, and illuminative dreams. This crystal boosts the intuition in a big way and even engenders an ease in past-life recollection.

## IRON PYRITE

Fool's gold! Some of my friends say I'm a magpie because I am so attracted to shiny objects. Let's count fool's gold among them. I don't care if it is a hundred times less valuable than actual gold, it is very pleasing to my magpie eyes, and every time I see it, I want to possess it. You'll be happy to know I have restrained myself (often with the help of friends) many times. Iron pyrite is usually the bright metallic yellow of its namesake but can also come in bright green and coppery colors, too. Mined in North America and South America, it is a crystal that has been mineralized, forming shiny cube clusters.

Iron pyrite enables the skin to ward off contaminants. It is a plus for the respiratory system and is said to aid oxygen flow. It also has a strong connection to the iron levels in the blood and therefore benefits the circulatory system. Many people get relief from digestive ailments, too.

I treasure iron pyrite for its nearly unmatched support to personal mental workings. It boosts creativity, intelligence, logic, and the ability to communicate and soothes fretfulness and angst. These crystal clusters radiate stability. Native Americans revered iron pyrite as a protective amulet. This money-bringing and creativity-boosting stone is a must for the studios and workstations of artists, musicians, writers, and anyone whose artistry provides income.

## *Tips 'n' Tricks*

### A BOX OF ROCKS

Keep a magic wishing box on your desk. Every so often look at it and make a wish upon your heart's desire. It's easy to make: Take a bowl or lidless box and fill it halfway with sand. Place these suggested wish stones in any arrangement you find pleasing:

- **agate** for a new home,
- **amethyst** for spirituality,
- **carnelian** or **lapis lazuli** for a job,
- **coral** for wanting children,
- **fool's gold** for money, and
- **rose quartz** for love.

### JADE

I can't help but marvel that I'm writing about jade on Chinese New Year. Jade is held in the highest regard by the Chinese and has been for thousands of years, thought to bring good luck and prosperity. Jade is a harbinger of purity and tranquillity. The Chinese so adore this stone that they carry little talismanic pieces with them everywhere they go. Other cultures—the Maori of New Zealand and the Japanese—also hold jade as blessed. Jade is a soft stone, perfect for carving. Both the Chinese and Japanese decorated royal personages with exquisite jade jewelry. Jade comes from Myanmar, Russia, Italy, China, and North and Central America. It is so affordable. I urge you to explore all the magical colors—yellow, orange, blue, red, purple, white, brown, and the classic jade green—and powers of positivity.

Jade brings with it the power of love and protection. It is also a dream stone, promoting prophetic and deeply meaningful dreams.

- **Purple** jade heals the broken heart, allowing understanding and acceptance in and pain and anger out. If you are going through a breakup, purple jade will help you with the heartache.
- **Green** jade is the counselor stone and can help relationships that aren't working become functional instead of dysfunctional; this shade is also a boon for the brain. Green jade helps with getting along.
- **Red** jade promotes the proper release of anger and also generates great sexual passion. Serve your lover a passion potion in a cup of carved red jade while wearing only red jade. Sparks will fly!
- **Blue** jade is a rock for patience and composure and for conveying a sense of control. Wear blue jade pendants for serenity.
- **Yellow** jade is for energy, simple joy, and maintaining a sense of being part of a greater whole. A yellow jade bracelet or ring will help you feel that all is well in your world.

Jadeite and nephrite are the two varieties of jade, with the far more translucent and rarer jadeite being the more popular. Their healing properties are very much the same, however, and the different colors manifest different curatives. All jade brings positive energy. In the year 2001, a 2,000-ton boulder of jade was discovered in the city Ptiakant in Myanmar—now that is a whole lotta love!

## JASPER

The authors of the Bible mentioned jasper quite a lot; their great city of heaven is reputed to have jasper walls. This opaque kind of chalcedony is a common stone here on Earth. In fact, it is found on every continent. It occurs in shades of brown, yellow, blue, green, and red, as well as combinations of these colors, often displayed in exquisite striations. Jasper has been ground up into powder and added to healing elixirs for thousands of years. The stone offers encouraging effects, but they tend to happen gradually over a long period of time. Patience is required. Jasper is an energy crystal and also a stone of sensuality, engendering immense ardor.

+ **Brown** jasper can connect you to the earth and also to past lives, helping with regressional memories and uncovering all patterns that have clung on from incarnation to incarnation. If you are interested in exploring previous incarnations, wear brown jasper rings or bracelets on your left arm and pay attention to your dreams, which will be revealed!

+ **Yellow** jasper is the spirit rock, an aid during any spiritual work. It is also a great stone to take on a trip, a traveler's support. Yellow jasper offers vigor and touches upon the endocrine system. Wear a yellow jasper ring on your right hand on your next trip and you will enjoy lively dreams.

+ **Blue** jasper impacts the sacral and heart chakras and makes travel in the astral plane possible. This is a powerfully mystical crystal. Blue jasper can put you into the spirit realm yet keep you anchored to the earthly plane. It is perfect for any soul work. If you want to embark on a new spiritual practice or even deepen your meditation, this gem will set you on the proper path.

+ **Green** jasper is great for the skin and for the mind; if you are thinking too much about any one thing, green jasper will dispel the obsession. Women, including myself, also value this shade because it prevents bloating. For clear skin and an even clearer mind, wear green jasper!

+ **Red** jasper can bring emotions that lie beneath the surface to the forefront for healing. This stone is connected strongly to the root chakra, the source of sexual energy and kundalini. If you would like to explore the sacred sexual practice of tantra, both partners could wear red jasper, the stone of passion. Red jasper can be a tool for rebirth and finding justice.

Jasper is a nurturing stone and can create a sense of wholeness through chakra alignment. I need to place jasper on my desk, as well, as it is a great organizational crystal and would help see all my various projects through to completion. This is a stone that balances the male and female energies. Jasper will ground you, and the lovely spectrum of shades can help you care for yourself, body and soul.

## JET

Jet is a stone but is organic—petrified wood found all over the world in deposits dating back to the Stone Age. It is a tough form of lignite coal that is polished to a glossy sheen, unlike ordinary coal. Jet is black and extremely hard. It has been with us since prehistory and was found to have been used for both tools and jewels in the caves ancient Europeans lived in.

Native Americans also wore jet in power amulets. Jet is an energy absorber and has been used as such for centuries; it has been used for many disparate cures, from insanity to the common cold. The absorbency, however, makes it truly great for dispelling fear, and though it obviously can't cure mental illness, it can help stabilize mood swings and stave off debilitating depression. Jet is used to

## *Tips 'n' Tricks*

### HOPE STONE

In this day and age of turbulence and chaos, you can use stone power to remain steadfast during the toughest times. Sky blue amazonite is the hope stone of ancient legend and can give you the fortitude to withstand any trials and tribulations.

treat headaches, edema, and epilepsy. Anyone who suffers from migraines should carry a jet amulet to ease both the pain and the fear around those difficult episodes. Jet is also a potent treatment for enhancing virility. The stone is best served by a silver mounting in jewelry. Jet is a useful dream stone and can send forewarning of sorrowful events. Despite that, jet is a stone of the positive, creating optimism and improved money energy.

 ## *Dream Crystals*

Crystals have been used for millennia for seeing into the future, long before crystal balls were first used for divination. Certain crystals are very powerful revelatory rocks, showing what is to come through dreams. In extremely rare cases, stones show the future through their shiny surfaces. Crystals are highly recommended as tools to use for calling up dreams; I slept with a garnet by my head last night to bring about an empowered state of mind and inspired visions. The appearance of stones, gems, and crystals in your dreams is deeply meaningful. If you are so lucky as to see light shining through a stone in a dream, you will soon be relieved of a problem or issue that has been plaguing you. Here is an age-old dream that rarely happens in the modern day but is a clear message from the unconscious mind: If you dream of jewels in a cave guarded by a dragon or other fantastical creatures, your spiritual side is longing to come out and be nourished and supported. Get thee to a retreat!

Here is a concise guide to the meaning of crystals appearing in your dreams:

- **Agate:** Beware of an impending rift between friends.
- **Amethyst:** Expect great news of a surprising nature.
- **Aquamarine:** Look forward to a very happy love life.
- **Bloodstone:** Watch out for unhappiness in love.
- **Diamond:** If you do not own any diamonds, anticipate a gain but less than expected. If you own diamonds, expect a loss.
- **Jade:** Await abundance and financial security.

- **Jet:** Strengthen for sorrowful news.
- **Lapis lazuli:** Have wisdom to remain flexible to change.
- **Onyx:** Fight procrastination due to fear of failure.
- **Opal:** Give or receive a valuable gift.
- **Quartz:** Brace for betrayal by a trusted friend or loved one.
- **Ruby:** Ignite great romantic passion.
- **Sapphire:** If you are wearing it in a dream, watch out for sudden urges. If another person is wearing it, get ready to gain recognition and status.

## KUNZITE

Perhaps the reason the pretty crystal kunzite hasn't reached great popularity is that its splintery nature makes it a real challenge to cut. This lesser-known stone is the pink variety of spodumene and is one of only two gems in this small family; the green hiddenite is the other. Mined in North America, Brazil, Myanmar, Afghanistan, and Madagascar, it has a striated surface and is translucent. Kunzite has different color intensities depending on the vantage point from which it is being viewed. Its deep pinkness is due to the mineral lithium it contains. If lithium sounds familiar, that's because it is. Lithium has been used widely in the treatment of mental illness. Kunzite is indeed a spirit-lifting, soothing stone and helps neutralize stress and prevent worry and fear. This pink stone can help you control your thoughts and have the ability to detach yourself from what bothers you. Kunzite is a heart opener and creates the condition for love. It is also beneficial to the blood and circulatory system. Kunzite can help anyone with substance-abuse issues or the proclivity toward addiction deal with such problems. Kunzite is another of the environmental stones that can absorb and block harmful radio waves. It will also help you feel and express your love for your significant other without feeling possessive and jealous.

## LABRADORITE

I LOVE labradorite. As I said before, I love shiny, glittery objects, but I have a special thing for iridescence. Plus, labradorite is a sleeping beauty. It can look as dull as dirt until you give it a closer examination; then you can see the glow under the surface. When cut and polished, it is fascinating and gorgeous, with an impressive light show including yellows, oranges, blues, and violets. Sometimes a single color takes the stage, and other times they perform all at once. In fact, the special play of light and color across the surface is called labradorescence. The effect is caused by lamellar intergrowths, which were produced inside the crystal while the crystal formed during a shift of temperature from extremely high to very low. Named for the place it was first found, Labrador, this loveliest of shiny objects can also be found in India, Finland, Russia, Newfoundland, and Madagascar.

As you might guess, this bluish feldspar is a soul stone with a very powerful light energy. It abets astral travel, the higher mind, and intelligence and is a favorite of mystics. It brings up nothing but the positive for the brain and consciousness and excises the lower energies of anxiety, stress, and negative thoughts. It is an aura cleanser and balancer. Labradorite, which used to be called spectrolite, also protects against aura leakage. This is a crystal to hold and keep with you during meditation for psychic flashes, much like the flashes of light from within the stone.

## LAPIS LAZULI

As long as I can remember, this has been one of my favorite stones. The mysterious blue and extremely compelling surface is like no other, both smooth and rough at the same time. Some lapis lazuli specimens are even flecked with fool's gold, pyrite, giving them an irresistible glitter. Still others are swirled with streaks of white calcite.

Through lapis, I feel a connection with all things ancient. I associate lapis lazuli with the Egyptians, but it is now most often found in Russia and Afghanistan. The Egyptians favored this handsome rock immensely, and it was their most highly regarded talisman, considered to be most magical. Lapis lazuli is the gateway to unlocking your own intuition and, as such, is invaluable.

As with any other crystal, it must be used with thoughtfulness and caution, but do double your vigilance with this one! It is one of the major mental stones; lapis lazuli is a thought amplifier very nearly second to none. Lapis also enhances psychic power and can open the third eye by being laid very briefly on your forehead in the place of the third eye.

In this day and age, almost all of us are overextended and become so busy that we get away from our core. There is a danger with this: We can get off track and stop living our lives—our lives are living us. We can get so caught up in the busyness of work and home and family obligations that we are not living out our destinies. Lapis lazuli is a stone that will help you always stay in touch with your essence, with who you are supposed to be becoming. Blue is always the color of peace, spirituality, and tranquillity. Lapis lazuli is a guide to be listened to in absolute stillness. In today's world of endless distraction, I urge you to dive into the pool of blue that is lapis lazuli and restore yourself. This gem will help you regain your balance. Lapis lazuli is such a powerful healer that it has even been used to dispel hallucinations.

Lapis is a cleansing stone, which is of great aid to the lungs, the blood, the liver, the kidneys, the nervous system, and the immune system. Lapis is also a great pain reliever and can simply be applied to the spot in need of relief. This gem has been used to treat migraines for centuries. According to sage wisdom that has been passed down about this special stone, lapis lazuli must be worn above the waist so that energy is passed upward. Wear it near the throat for the best effect.

## Tips 'n' Tricks

### LAPIS LEDGER

The power of lapis lazuli directly reflects the energy of the person who wears it. I suggest keeping a record of what happens in your life when you wear it, a sort of lapis lazuli progress report. It might end up being a series of extraordinary stories!

### MAGNETITE

This gray or dark brown stone is also known as lodestone, a poetic name I much prefer. It has a major quantity of iron and is, as the name implies, very magnetic. The ancients called it lodestone, although Plato himself wrote that it was "the heraclean stone." All iron-based crystals are considered to be very helpful to the blood and the circulatory system. Magnet therapy has come into vogue in the last twenty years and is becoming pretty commonplace nowadays. Even athletes and physicians are trying magnetic therapy, and any controversy about this onetime New Age healing method is fading thanks to the many positive endorsements.

### MALACHITE

I received a beautiful malachite heart from my mother and father for Christmas this year—how I treasure it! Malachite has always been a connection to the Divine, especially divine inspiration. Malachite, named for the Greek word *mallow* (green herb), is formed from copper ore and frequently occurs in conjunction with chrysocolla and azurite. Malachite is a lovely green blue in color and has endless patterned bands. No two pieces of malachite are ever alike. Malachite was associated with royals and high priests and priestesses in ancient times. They loved to adorn their bodies, their homes, and their temples with this special stone. They would have entire tables and chairs and altars. One would certainly feel like a king or queen when dining from a malachite table! Even still, some of the largest sheets found in South Africa, Zambia, Zaire, Russia, and Romania are fashioned into small boxes, bowls, and obelisks.

Malachite can help you connect to your place in the Divine Plan. Malachite draws out old patterns and thoughts. It will aid in clearing away the deadwood from your life and your psyche. It offers psychic protection, too. This green grounding stone will also get you more in touch with the earth and more grounded as a person—more stable. As with most green stones, it has to do with prosperity, abundance, and money. Malachite will awaken your creativity. If you are allowing others to benefit from your creativity, this stone will help stop that draining in its tracks. Malachite requires extra care in its use because it amplifies whatever energies are already there. If anger, suffering, and deceit are present, these qualities could inadvertently be increased by malachite. Basically, malachite is really useful only for people who are typically helpful and happy. It is best for

*Tips 'n' Tricks*

## MALACHITE BONE SOOTHER

One healer recommends this malachite bone cure: Using tape or a soft cord, create a band with a small piece of malachite. Tape or wrap the band to the injured or bruised area and leave it overnight. The benefits should start within one day as the inflammation is greatly eased by the miraculous coppery green crystal. I have a bad ankle from a really bad sprain and a subsequent really bad break, and my malachite ankle band is invaluable when the ache-inducing rain is coming on.

children, really. One theory is that malachite is still evolving and is becoming a master key for the future.

Malachite helps with maintaining boundaries and comes highly recommended for that purpose by many healers. Malachite can help restore anyone who is suffering from burnout. Those who do psychic work and healing are among those who are affected by this most severely, so they need to keep malachite nearby for rejuvenation. Malachite opens the heart and throat chakras and rebalances the solar plexus, enabling realignment of the psychic and etheric bodies. Malachite is best used as a ring on your right hand. Malachite is used to ward off insanity and has been used both as an eye remedy and as a cosmetic by the unstoppable Egyptians. I shudder to think of the Egyptian elixirs involving malachite, many recipes for which they left behind on papyrus; they are very likely extremely toxic. Please avoid any malachite elixirs!

## MOONSTONE

This milky, bluish white feldspar gemstone cut from albite is beloved the world over for its pleasant and somewhat mysterious smooth surface. Moonstone is quite obviously connected to the moon and is as soothing to the psyche as it is pleasing for the eye. The gem is associated with sensitivity, psychic ability, loyalty, sleep and dreams, emotional balance, and femininity. Moonstone is related to all the feminine organs and also the cleansing organs, especially the skin. This stone has a very rare ability to help with eating disorders, particularly overeating. It can calm the stomach and adjust the vibrations so you are directed to eat the proper amount in the future. Moonstone opens the heart chakra and, very importantly, helps overcome any anger or hard emotions toward the self. Pagans have seen this as a Goddess crystal for millennia and see it as a source for nurturing, wisdom, and intuition. A moonstone is a powerfully protective and loving talisman for a pregnant woman. In India, moonstone is sacred and very lucky but is even more valued in the subcontinent because it helps make you more spiritual. Moonstone is at its very best on your behalf if worn in a ring with a silver setting.

## MORGANITE

Named after J. P. Morgan, one of the richest American men of his time, this is really a pink beryl and occurs in Brazil, Russia, and North America. It deserves its own mention since it is a crystal with powerful love energy. Morganite is also wonderfully beneficial to the nerves and is a calming crystal. But the greatest gift this gem can give you is to bring love into your life and keep it there.

*Tips 'n' Tricks*

### POLISH YOUR PERCEPTIONS

So what do you do if you are attracted to all the wonderful qualities I just stated are inherent in the mysterious, watery green malachite but are afraid of the negativity-amplifying aspect? Go for this fairly commonplace natural merging of malachite and azurite becoming popularly known as azur-malachite. It is a similarly lovely green blue and a real helper crystal. Azurite has the incredible ability to help us all integrate unacknowledged beliefs, and malachite is a creativity crystal, so when these two stones occur together, their combined power enables us to handle the hardest truths about ourselves.

Whereas malachite is so powerful by itself that it can cause heart palpitations among more sensitive souls, the combined stone is very gentle and peaceful. What Aldous Huxley wrote about, cleansing the doors of perception, can happen with azur-malachite!

## RELATIONSHIP RESCUE

If you and your mate are simply not getting along of late, turn to this romantic remedy rock: moonstone. Moonstone can reunite loved ones who have parted in anger. This lovely, shimmering stone also imparts luck in love. Keep moonstone around, by all means!

## MUSCOVITE

Muscovite, mined in Switzerland, Austria, and the Czech Republic and found first in Russia, from whence it takes its name (after the city Moscow), is fairly common. It often comes in sheets of mica that can be clear and translucent or a pearly white, gray, pale pink, yellow, rose red, or violet. At one time, sheets of muscovite were used in the kitchen over windows. While it is most frequently an ordinary rock, it can occur as a gem; of particular note is the rare Brazilian twin variety that forms five-pointed stars and is referred to as star muscovite. There is also an emerald green specimen called fuchsite.

Muscovite is a problem-solving crystal. It also has a rare and wonderful quality in that it facilitates astral travel and astral projection. This is a visionary stone and can put you in contact with the angelic realm so you can call on your guardian angels to come to your aid. Muscovite helps us all to take a deep look inside and see how we are missing out on important messages and are unaware of certain behaviors and projections we are putting out unconsciously. Though this can be tough work, this kind of self-examination is essential for true soul growth. Muscovite also gives the inner grit to make changes based on this new information about the self.

## OBSIDIAN

This black volcanic glass is found the world over. Obsidian was an important tool for prehistoric peoples, who used it for knives, mirrors, bowls, and jewelry. Obsidian is most often thought of as a pure, glassy black, but it can also have milky white stripes or flecks. Rainbow obsidian, a spiritual love crystal, is especially beautiful, with peacock-colored gradations. And dark red mahogany obsidian is a true gift, as it puts you in touch with your life's very purpose. Native Americans valued obsidian immensely for its eagle-eye vision power, which they believed was good for the eyes as well as for seeing within. Shamans still hold obsidian in the highest regard, and it has come to be an invaluable aid in prophesying.

Obsidian is a protector and absorbs and keeps away negativity. It is also a rock with very direct energies and will help with great immediacy. Very sensitive people should keep obsidian around their homes and offices. This is a letting-go stone and will get rid of old patterns, old thoughts, a lingering torch for an old flame, or whatever you need to be over and done with. It gives you the get-up-and-go to get on with your life—to travel and explore and grow. Don't wear or keep obsidian around all the time, though, as you will wear yourself and the stone out!

*Tips 'n' Tricks*

### MAGICAL MARCASITE SCRYING RING

Did you know that lovely marcasite is really hematite? Thank heavens it has made a fashion comeback of late and is commonly available in inexpensive jewelry. This powerful seer stone can be used for a quick scrying. Look at your marcasite ring and then close your eyes and see what flashes into your mind.

## OPAL FIRE POWER

Opal is best worn as a pinkie ring. It is also a popular engagement ring, as it is a symbol of faithfulness and is effective in bringing stability and longevity to relationships. Fire opal is good for business by promoting positive action and prosperity. Hold your opal in your right hand and your wishes will be granted!

## ONYX

Onyx has a lot of earth energy. This stone can come in many colors—from white to black with every shade in between, including pink, red, yellow, and brown. It is so common that it is often used as building material. I would think it would be interesting to live in a building made of onyx since this stone holds memories and secrets! Onyx retains the physical record of what happens around it; therefore, it is a story stone. Onyx is superstable and shares this strength with people who need it. It is particularly good for athletes and people who do physical labor. Healers recommend that onyx be worn *only* on the left side of the body or on a chain so that it hangs at the center of the body in the heart and solar plexus area. Onyx is best at relieving stress and quieting the mind.

This is a generous rock in that it creates goodwill and self-confidence. If you have an occasion that makes you nervous, or a very thorny and difficult task at hand, you should adorn yourself with an onyx ring, bracelet, or pendant, and things will go much better and you will feel more optimistic about them. Onyx is good for issues with the skeleton, the teeth, and the bones. Be careful about wearing onyx as a choker, as this is believed to dampen the heat of passion in romantic matters!

## OPAL

This gem can light the inner fire of your spirituality. One of the seven sacred stones of the Cherokee people, opal is a favorite of many for its fiery and glinting opacity. The milky white stone seems to have an ever changing rainbow of colors inside; this is due to a high percentage of water in its makeup. This gem has one of the best spectral displays of any stone, and the opalescence is the result of many layers of precipitated silica balls in a jelly-like watery mass.

There are three different kinds of opals: precious opal, with the telltale flashes of fire; fire opal, in the reddish yellow color; and common opal, with the rather unfortunate-sounding name of potch. Black opal is the rarest and most desirable of the precious opals, and the highest grade comes from one place in Australia, Lightning Ridge.

Although opals are semiprecious gems, their name comes from the Latin word *opalus,* meaning "precious stone." They are among the more sensitive gemstones. They need TLC and can be irrevocably damaged by exposure to heat and chemicals. In addition, they can lose their large water content if they are cracked or damaged. Opals need to be approached with very nearly the same level of caution in terms of using them for energy and healing work, as they can easily diffuse personal energies.

Opals can help you if you want to get the special attention of a certain someone or if you have to give a speech or presentation. Opal is one of the rare stones that has both male and female energies within; it contains the energy of the sun *and* the moon. The fiery flashes generate flashes of intuition and of inspiration. Opals can facilitate wonderful dreams and positive change. They can bring submerged feelings and trapped emotions to the surface and can help uptight individuals get in touch with their emotions and loosen up.

# PEARL

Pearls have long been cherished as symbols of perfection and purity. Pearls shimmer with beauty and have also come to represent riches and elegance. To me, pearls signify self-containment. This is another of the gems and crystals formed from organic origins; it starts as a lowly secretion coating an irritating grain of sand inside a freshwater or marine mollusk shell. Pearls are usually the much-loved, lustrous whitish color but can be a rainbow of shades, including pink, violet, black, gray, tan, and gold, with many other subtle permutations.

Throughout human history, pearls have fascinated and have been used as a favored adornment. People so lusted after them that they began introducing sand into oysters to force pearl production, resulting in the cultured pearls we see on the market today. For myself, I prefer the more oddly shaped freshwater pearls. Sadly, natural pearls have become nearly nonexistent due to the overheated oceans of the world and industrial pollution.

Pearls have affinities to the moon, femininity, and fertility, and they are a sacred symbol for pregnant women. The great tradition of pearls, especially in Asia, was that they represented modesty and wholesomeness. Pearls are truly soothing. That is why they exist in the first place—for soothing the irritated shellfish. They are an excellent helpmate in any stress-related illness and are good for stomachaches, ulcers, hypertension, headaches, and fatigue.

Pearls amplify energy and are especially good in combination with emeralds and diamonds. They are environmentally sensitive and pick up vibrations from the person wearing them. What is more, they remember the feeling (positive or negative), hold it inside, and then emanate it. If you are in a sad or bad mood, remove your pearls so you don't unknowingly keep that negativity hanging around you. By the same token, do not ever loan your pearls.

## PERIDOT

Pretty, pale green peridot is the gem variety of olivine. Peridot has been mined as a gemstone for more than 4,000 years, and until recently, the best-quality stones came from Egypt. Now, Arizona has lovely specimens, and Pakistan may have the world's finest-quality peridot at this point. Peridot has a nearly unmatched clarity and is considered a visionary stone. It helps us connect to our higher life purpose and achieve a deeper soul connection.

Peridot is a real confidence booster, too. It cuts through the clouds and helps achieve quick results. If you are shy and slow moving, peridot may make things happen a little too quickly for your comfort level. You should also get really clear about what you truly want. If you are confused about your worldly goals, this is not the stone for you!

Peridot helps release toxins and brings issues to the surface so they can be cleared away. This gem is peerless for the release of anger. The clarity of peridot will help you realize clarity in your sphere, as well. Peridot is good for the skin and is a stomach soother.

*Tips 'n' Tricks*

### COVER-ALL-THE-BASES CRYSTAL

If you are keeping yourself on a strict budget, get one piece of jewelry that will help you in nearly every area of your life—health, wealth, love, family, career, travel, friendship, and creativity. Go to the nearest Chinatown, where the prices are right, and get a bracelet featuring multiple hues of jade. One-stop shopping to a better life now!

## PYROLUSITE

This stone has an attractive and dramatic name, from the Greek words *pyr* (fire) and *lousis* (washing). The ancients must have thought pyrolusite looked as if it had been washed by fire. Pyrolusite is the thin, fan-shaped black-and-white oxide of manganese usually found at the bottom of a bog or on the ocean floor. It can also grow in the cracks between rocks, in which case it forms lovely, fern-like dendrite crusts.

Pyrolusite is amazing for transformation. It helps get rid of buried emotions and anything that might be interfering with spiritual growth. Pyrolusite will get to the root of a problem and dislodge it. This rock defends the etheric body, or aura, from negative energy and bad energy. Pyrolusite is also good for the metabolism and is helpful for treating bronchitis. Pyrolusite is a stabilizing stone that is excellent for relationships and stimulates the sensual side of life. It is a stone favored by shamans.

## QUARTZ

Entire books could be, and doubtless have been, written about quartz, which is actually an entire family of stones. Quartz is made up mostly of silicon dioxide, making it the salt of the earth. Crystals of quartz can be found in every imaginable shape and shade and quite often even have other minerals encased inside them. Quartz is one crystal embraced by the scientific community and is used in a lot of technology and the manufacturing of products from computers to clocks to power tools. Rock crystal, or white quartz, is commonly available and is a truly terrific healer. Light passes through this stone quite easily, making it a balancer and purifier.

Rock crystal has the amazing ability to vibrate with all of the colors of the spectrum and all frequencies, so it can be healing to all seven chakras. Rock crystal will also facilitate personal growth by amplifying whatever energy is already there. Any problems that need to be worked out will present themselves for fixing. Rock crystal clears away blockages that lead to health problems, as well.

Rock crystal is really great for meditation and can guide you on your quest for enlightenment. This rock will help you tune into your own vibration and help exclude any interference, so you can reach a deep level of consciousness.

The following stones are members of the quartz family, and many are explained in their own sections of this descriptionary:

| | | |
|---|---|---|
| + agate | + chalcedony | + moss agate |
| + amethyst | + chrysoprase | + onyx |
| + aventurine | + citrine | + opal |
| + basanite | + dendritic agate | + rose quartz |
| + bloodstone | + flint | + rutilated quartz |
| + blue quartz | + fossilized wood | + sard |
| + carnelian | + hawk's-eye | + smoky quartz |
| + cat's-eye | + jasper | + tiger's-eye |

## Blue Quartz

An uncommon stone found occasionally in Siberia, North America, and Brazil, blue quartz, also known as dumortierite, ranges from a grayish blue to pale blue to lavender in color. It is found only in very old rock formations because the process by which it gains its color is very slow and takes many millennia to be completed.

Blue quartz is best for the upper torso and is also a boost to the bloodstream and the body's immune system. Blue is the color of spirit, and this is a wonderful meditation crystal for spirit work. It is a stone of hope, of calm, and of soul. Blue quartz is a mental stone, as well, and can help with self-discipline, organizational skills, and studying. This crystal aids the throat chakra and therefore aids in communication, helping you to speak your truth—and speak it well.

 *Syberian Blue*

One type of blue quartz I have recently become fascinated with is called the Flower of Life and comes from cold Siberia. This is a special cut that enhances the beneficial energies inherent in the crystal and causes energy to spiral through the crystal itself and get amplified every time it reverberates against a facet in the cut. Following the principles of sacred geometry, each side is cut into a six-petaled flower, creating a stunning twelve-pointed star. Additionally, this blue quartz carries the *blue ray*, which touches upon the throat and the third eye, awakening powerful intuition and the ability to communicate the visions.

### Rose Quartz

No other mineral has a color anything like the pink and rose colors of rose quartz, which are caused by titanium and iron. Rose quartz, thankfully, comes in large enough masses that it has been used in many sacred statues, obelisks, and spheres. Although these crystals come from India, Madagascar, Germany, and North America, the best specimens come from mineral-rich Brazil.

A truly extraordinary type of rose quartz is the kind with rutile needles that create a gorgeous star effect. I aim to get one of these, perhaps to celebrate and mark the publication of this gem book! Rose quartz is an emotion stone and is particularly good for matters of the heart. It is gently soothing, slowly allowing the release of hurt and negative feelings and memories. I strongly recommend keeping pieces at home and at work where you can see them and instantly get a lift every time you look at your chunks of love.

Rose quartz engenders self-love, which we must have before we can really love anyone else. Self-forgiveness and self-acceptance are made possible with rose quartz meditation. I have a very large piece with a light centered at the base of my bed, and the warm pink glow immediately makes the room a comforting cocoon. The heat of the bulb also causes the stone to release cheery negative ions into my bedroom. Rose quartz is a crystal of tenderness, nurturing, compassion, sympathy, and faith.

This rock has healing power over the heart and the circulatory system, naturally, as well as the reproductive and cleansing organs. Traditionally, rose quartz is believed to abet fertility. It is especially good for sensitive souls—artists, musicians, writers, poets, and anyone of a gentle and receptive nature.

## Rutilated Quartz

Rutiles are the needle-like inclusions in minerals. Native Americans, who teach that spiders are the weavers of the world, saw the rutiles inside the quartz as the web of the spider, a tool for weaving our dreams into reality. Therefore, rutilated quartz is the crystal of manifestation, bringing ideas and dreams into the world in which we live. I love rutilated quartz and always have; one of my favorite pieces is a big pendant set in silver on a leather strap that I can adjust to whatever necklace length I need on any given day.

The rutiles are not only beautiful and mysterious looking; they also amplify healing. These inclusions can occur in almost any kind of quartz, and they will intensify the healing properties specific to that stone. Rutilated quartz is the healers' healer, helping them uncover the true causes of illness. Many healers have found that rutilated quartz has the power to regenerate the body's tissues and to help nutritional supplements and herbs to do their jobs better. The crystal is invaluable for the respiratory system and is an immune system booster, too. It is also said to slow the aging process.

## Smoky Quartz

Smoky quartz, like many other brown stones, is a grounding crystal and affects the parts of the body closest to the earth—the lower torso and the root chakra. As a healer, smoky quartz helps the kidneys, abdomen, pancreas, and sexual organs. It can help a person stuck in a decadent cycle of sexual gratification and promiscuity break out of that meaningless cycle toward real love.

I like how smoky quartz facilitates the creation and achievement of business goals as well as higher personal aspirations. Smoky quartz is one of the only crystals I know that can generate an attitude of patience and fortitude. This dark stone also helps with perspicacity and perseverance—slowly but surely you can get to the top of the mountain! Smoky quartz is calming and is a wonderful antidepressant stone. In the same vein, it abets issues of obsessiveness and addiction and can help people struggling with codependency. Smoky quartz also helps people get over negative emotions such as fear, anger, and jealousy. This stone can point out what is important in your life and what is not; it will lead you in overcoming the emotional blocks that stop you from prioritizing your wants and needs. Smoky quartz will move through your lower mind and help your soul grow toward a higher mind and new stages of creativity and inspiration. As an elixir, smoky quartz is superb for radiation illnesses.

This stone is great in combination with these relatives in the quartz family: rose quartz, citrine, and amethyst. If you work with this trinity of crystals, you can balance female and male energies—the yin and yang. I find that moldavite is rather ungrounding for me, but smoky quartz can ameliorate that effect and get my feet back on the earth.

## RHODOCHROSITE

The name simply means "rose-colored," and the color is astounding. This stone seems as if it is lit from within. It is one of the newer crystals on the scene, coming from Russia and North America. Rhodochrosite is imminently appealing, with its stripes of pink and sometimes orange.

Rhodochrosite is a love stone that will enable anyone who believes they have never truly felt or experienced real love to find it. I heard and read about some people gleaning much good from it during the aftermath of 9/11. It functions as a heart-chakra opener that brings compassion and expands consciousness. One fascinating legend associated with rhodochrosite is that it can connect you to your soul mate if used in meditation. This is also a crystal that helps with the healing power of forgiveness. It also helps overcome irrationality and can prevent a mental breakdown. I think my favorite feature of rhodochrosite is that it overcomes a poor memory. So, this rose-colored beauty banishes forgetfulness and promotes forgiveness—what a nice combination. Healers also work with this stone for respiratory disease. It has a warm energy that is very good for the body.

This striking stone is also invaluable for overcoming fear and paranoia (mental unease). Rhodochrosite abets a more positive world view. One of the simplest and best aspects of this crystal is that it will help you to sleep more peacefully, shoving apprehension, worry, and woe out of your mind so you can heal body and soul. Your dreams will be positive, too. This is a remarkable stone for affirming the self, allowing absolute self-acceptance and self-forgiveness. Rhodochrosite brings together the spiritual plane and the material place. The crystal is important because it permits the heart to feel hurt and pain deeply, and this processing of emotions nurtures growth.

## RHODONITE

Musicians, sound technicians, and singers love this heart-chakra crystal for its peerless capacity to help with hearing and listening. Rhodonite is sometimes confused with the rosy pink crystal rhodochrosite, but it is identifiably different in that it has white streaks or black mottling. Like many other pink stones, however, it is a love stone and a nurturing stone, and has a specialty: It is tremendous for dealing with the pain and suffering associated with grief and the loss of a loved one. This is a rock that will enable anyone to become more heart centered while stabilizing the emotions. This stone also assists by revealing both sides of an issue for clear thinking and real fairness in decision making. Rhodonite aligns the physical, emotional, and mental facets of your entire being and brings balance to them. If you are feeling ungrounded and a bit scattered, this crystal will soothe and uplift. Rhodonite can help you attain your greatest potential. This is a confidence crystal. The highest-grade gem form of rhodonite awakens the intuition.

Found in India, Japan, Spain, North America, Brazil, and Russia, this rock can also come in darker colors ranging from red to brown. As a healer, rhodonite alleviates the shock that accompanies a grievous loss. It is also used for issues involving the ears and hearing and is said to be very good for bone growth. Rhodonite helps build a healthy emotional foundation, making for a stronger personality and stronger person.

Rhodonite is a favorite carving stone in Russia; it was used for the sarcophagi of czars and emperors and is still popular as an Easter egg carving exchanged among the children of that country. I think the best and highest use of rhodonite is for healing old emotional wounds and scars, and growing from the experience. If you are feeling low-grade anxiety, this is an excellent crystal to carry in your pocket as a touchstone.

## RUBY

This gem is ruled by the energy of the sun and was considered to be the stone of nobility. One of the most precious of all gems, ruby is at least as valuable as diamond—and is more valuable than diamond if it is unflawed. The red beauty is especially revered in China and India, where it is seen as a harbinger of health and happiness. In days long past, both these countries believed that a fading of the stone warned of impending problems. Like most other stones in the pink and red side of the spectrum, ruby is a heart stone and corresponds strongly with this chakra. Ruby heals the heart and carries the red ray of emotional wellness through the expression of love. This is a divine energy and as such there is a striving for the highest love vibration. Ruby brings joy into your life and gives you permission to follow your bliss.

Most commonly found in India, Sri Lanka, and North America, this jewel comes in a range of colors, from a really vivid red to a deep purplish crimson. The most valuable occurrence of this precious stone is the delicate rose color. You should be careful before selecting any ruby, as this gem is another energy amplifier. Ruby will magnify whatever energy is there to begin with, whether it is positive or negative. Its energy is extremely intense. Ruby's red color can quickly give rise to passions of a romantic and sexual nature as well as of anger and rage. You must bear this in mind when wearing ruby and remain conscious of your feelings.

People who do energy work and healing say that this gem can fill in and repair holes in the aura. Ruby affects the root chakra and is therefore connected to our most primal drives as humans—sex and survival. Ruby is a stone of loyalty, confidence, and courage. It will protect you. If you are exhausted, this wonder worker will replenish your drained chi and restore you to peak levels of vitality, strength, and stamina. Ruby is also said to eliminate blockages of the reproductive system and encourage healthy energy flow. It is even good for hypoglycemia.

I love this jewel because it helps overcome and eradicate negative thought patterns and habits. Ruby holds the singular power of love for the self and for others. If set in white or yellow gold, ruby's regenerative love power is greatly enhanced.

  ## How to Tell a Ruby Is Real, India Style

If you place a real ruby in a glass jar, red light will emanate from the jar. If pearls are put together with a real ruby on a silver platter, the silver will appear black, the pearls will take on a red sheen, and the ruby will glow with a brilliant fire. If you place a genuine ruby on an unopened lotus bud, the lotus will bloom almost immediately.

Good rubies are smooth, lustrous, extremely hard, brilliant, and transparent. Lesser-quality rubies are

- bubbled or dirty, which reduces the effectiveness of the gem;
- dull, which causes problems with male relatives, especially brothers;
- fragile, which portends lightning;
- cracked, which brings bad luck; or
- brittle, which causes difficulty in bearing male children.

## SAPPHIRE

The word sapphire has several origins, among them the Greek word *sapphiros,* meaning "beloved of Saturn," and indeed this is one of the most beloved stones in the universe. Gorgeous one and all, sapphires are usually thought of as blue but also come in gray, black, green, orange, pink, and white. Sapphires are found in Australia, India, and North America and are held in reverence the world over. I believe the healing power of a true blue sapphire to be a great gift to humanity, and will begin there. The dark blue sapphire, which looks like the inky blue night sky, is a creativity crystal. It also instills deep loyalty and close, long-lasting bonds between people.

Blue sapphire carries the blue ray of harmony, nourishing the mind, giving perspective, and putting the thoughts in order. Blue sapphire also increases mental flexibility and helps an individual achieve mastery of the self—mind, body, and spirit. Sapphire is a simple light on this most complicated thing, the human mind, with its myriad levels and endless new thoughts. On a soul level, sapphire is about clearing and focusing the mind. Discernment, deciding what to process and what to filter out and let go of, is the key to soul growth.

Sapphire is best worn as a necklace so it is closer to your head. The collective wisdom of healers tells us that a short necklace is even better because it connects with the throat chakra more quickly and has more immediate and more powerful effects. The throat chakra also corresponds with the blue ray. Many practitioners speak of cases in which the senses of sight and hearing became keener after exposure to blue sapphire.

You should not wear sapphire, especially large stones, too frequently, as they can begin to drain energy. Sometimes the body will throw up resistance to too much change too rapidly. The healing ray of sapphire will cause a mental dumping of unnecessary baggage, which could lead to spaciness. Do watch for this, as it is a sign that you need to stop wearing your sapphire for a week, at least. With blue sapphire, the color and clarity greatly impact its healing abilities. You will want your jeweler or gem dealer to allow you to look under the microscope to see if there is any black hue in the blue. If so, do not buy this stone; it will have no healing influence at all. Look for a true blue, a rich hue that's neither too indigo nor too purple nor too pale.

The gemologist's term "candescence" comes from the word "incandescence," meaning the level of light glow inherent in a stone. Not all stones possess candescence, but blue sapphire possesses nearly the highest level, giving this gem the ability to infuse us with the healing blue ray. My absolute favorite aspect of blue sapphire as a gem is that it is a direct way to get in touch with your spirit.

- ✦ **Dark blue** sapphire brings serenity and inner peace. This is a real tool for deep meditation. This gem also helps avoid negative energy and can help get rid of it. This particular sapphire frees you from perplexity in regard to your soul mission in this life; it helps you to know your true values and who you are at the deepest level.

- ✦ **Light blue** sapphire is a stone of inspiration, bringing new ideas and thought patterns. This blessed crystal also creates a feeling of excitement and fullness in daily living. This stone can reignite your lust for life!

- ✦ **Green** sapphire is a lucky gem. It is supposed to be good for your eyes and vision. A green sapphire will help you to remember your dreams more vividly. Wear this heart-chakra opener as a ring touching the skin and it will bring loyal love and friendship into your life. Additionally, this jewel smooths your way through life, clearing obstacles out of your path.

- ✦ **Lilac** sapphire is the stone for artistic and innovative people; it can eradicate any creative blocks and allow the free flow of ideas and motivation.

- **Orange** sapphire is a truth stone, allowing nothing but profound, base-level reality. If you suffer from illusory thinking or denial, this gem will cut right through that and help you see things just as they are. Orange sapphire is good for researchers, scholars, teachers, investigative journalists, and writers.

- **Pink** sapphire is a stone of surrender. This gem connotes higher love and infuses a sense of the greater good. Pink sapphire will help you deal with control issues and allow you to cooperate better with others. This rock reminds you that you don't have to do it all by yourself.

- **Purple** sapphire is a spiritual stone, a gem of awakening, raising kundalini energy. This is a wonderful tool for contemplation and meditation. Purple sapphire also kindles the crown chakra.

- **White** sapphire is a terrific stone of self-protection. This is good for anyone with issues of codependence or martyrdom. If you put yourself last, then get a white sapphire (your first act of putting yourself first) and be good to yourself. Caring for yourself physically, emotionally, and spiritually will make for a better world because there is a better you in it!

- **Black** sapphire is absorptive and draws harm away from the wearer. This is the most protective of all the sapphire family. Black sapphire also lends you confidence that comes from the intelligence inherent in the body. Wearing this stone will make you more sure of your hunches and intuition. This is a stone of steadiness and is great to wear on job interviews—you will get the job and keep it!

- **Yellow** sapphire, associated with Ganesh, the Hindu god of abundance and prosperity, is a wonderful stone of knowledge, for inner knowing and trust in that. This bright gem is also great for the memory and retention

of what you are learning. If you are wearing it for healing and
the intellectual stimulation it offers, the actual stone should touch
your finger.

## SARDONYX

There is a saying about sardonyx that for whoever wears it, "stupidity will be
eliminated." It is also reputed to be a cure for tumors and beneficial to bones.
Edgar Cayce appreciated it as a means to gain greater self-control. Sardonyx
makes speakers more eloquent. It is also a crystal to use if you are struggling with
depression.

This type of quartz is a real eye-catcher; sardonyx is a layered form of
chalcedony that usually appears as alternating stripes of white or black onyx in
combination with reddish brown chalcedony, or sard. This is a very popular
stone for carving into beads, cameos, and intaglios. Historically, women wore
sardonyx to attract a faithful lover. Roman soldiers preferred sardonyx with the
god of war, Mars, or the great hero Hercules carved into it for valor.

This stone derives its exotic-sounding name from the Greek work *sard*,
for Sardis, the capital city of the Asia Minor country Lydia. Mentioned in the
Bible, it was designated to be the fifth foundation stone of Jerusalem and was
associated with the Apostle Paul. It is now mined in Brazil, India, and Russia, in
addition to Asia Minor. In ancient times, sardonyx was valued for courageous
fighting spirit and lust for combat. It is great for explorers and those engaged in
uncovering new territories. This is a crystal business executives should wear. In
addition to being smarter and tumor-free, you can also drive away evil spirits
and keep dark sorcerers at bay with this handy crystal. Here is a curious bit
of lore: Any woman who owns sardonyx but neglects to wear it will be lonely.
On the other side, it brings conjugal bliss and good fortune.

## SELENITE

Here we have an angelic stone, one that can help you tune into your guardian angels and discover the real reason you are here on Earth—the divine purpose for your existence. Named for the moon, this white, glowing lucky stone is gypsum and must be handled carefully, as it is partially water soluble. Egyptians favored this white stone as an amulet. This is a great calmer and is magnificent for mental focus. As a chakra healer, selenite helps rid unhealthy and negative thoughts, yours or others', from your mind and etheric body. This stone can also be placed over the third eye to access stored information about your past lives. Selenite, with its white swirls, can give an enormous boost to creative visualization. In the same way this crystal retains, it is good for letting go and helps you forgive. Selenite can also be used for healing of the nerves, reproductive organs, and spine, lending flexibility. It is a record-keeping stone and carries information from the centuries on Earth it has witnessed. It can be a most auspicious crystal ball for gazing. A rare kind of selenite is gold selenite from Australia. It is good for grounding.

## SERPENTINE

Called Connemara by the Celts, serpentine is a favorite jewel, typically a green or brownish yellow stone. Found in North America and Europe, Italians have a fable that green serpentine can protect from snakebite. There was also a superstition about leaving serpentine in its natural state and not allowing tools, especially iron, to touch the stone. An exceptional healer, it is a detoxifier. Serpentine helps one to get more in control of life, more together. This is also a psychic stone and helps you get in touch with spirits. Serpentine is another memory rock, helping you access past reincarnations in order to bring wisdom you need for *this* life.

## SUGILITE

Like many other purple crystals, sugilite is both a spiritual stone and a mental stone. In fact, it helps you understand the effect your mind has on your body. Sugilite can help with learning disorders and remove blocks that prevent new patterns of thought. This rock is good for teachers and students, as it not only clears the paths in the brain but also creates an atmosphere of loving under-standing. It can be quite effective when dealing with autism. A gorgeous series of deep purple bands of color, this South African stone, also called luvulite, signi-fies the highest state of spiritual love. Another forgiveness and letting-go stone, sugilite is so powerful that it can help with channeling. Placed on the third-eye area, sugilite alleviates sadness and despondency. Immensely positive, sugilite protects your very soul from the frustration and disillusionment of this world.

As a healer, it dispels headaches and gently draws pain out of afflicted areas, bringing respite to inflammations, toxicity, and stress-related illness. Sugilite has been used to great effect to ease the discomfort of those suffering from can-cer. It is wonderful when a stone helps with both physical and emotional issues, as does sugilite. This stone absorbs anger, hurts, and energies that you have unwittingly picked up and are draining you. If you have problems with jealousy, this is the perfect stone to help you rise above any pettiness and bring out your best side in relationships. I love that sugilite creates a sense of belonging for those who always felt like outsiders.

## TOPAZ

Topaz is a teacher crystal, showing us how to love. This is the stone of true love and success and is fantastic for confidence and creativity. Topaz is an aura cleanser and helps overcome negativity, replacing it with a sense of joy, abundance, and love. From its facets, topaz even has a charge, both negative and positive; you can see and feel the charge if you rub the stone. Topaz occurs naturally in a golden yellow but can also come in blue, reddish blue, brown, green, light pink, and clear. It is found in many parts of the world, including Zimbabwe, Ireland, Russia, Burma, South Africa, Brazil, and California. Topaz is often discovered as worn water pebbles downstream from an underground cache of ore.

Topaz works through the laws of attraction and manifestation. Creative visualization and meditation with topaz on what you really want and believe is right for you is very potent. Set in a silver wand, topaz is a tremendous abundance tool, connecting to the great source of life, energy, and love. You will find that topaz makes you more sure of your intuitions. The bushmen of Africa used topaz ceremonially for sending their brethren to the next world and for healing.

When meditating with topaz, imagine that you are holding the very energy of the sun—warm, healing, and benevolent. If you are tapped out, burned-out, and at your lowest ebb, topaz will generate rays of replenishment to recharge you and get you back up to a good energy level. Topaz relaxes at the same time that it refills; it "coats" your nervous system so you feel comfortable and ready for anything. Topaz will help you see your real goals in this life and will even illuminate the path to getting there. Topaz is a generosity generator, and you will want to give unto another with no expectations of getting anything back. Yellow topaz attracts advantageous people into your life if worn on the ring finger. Blue topaz stimulates the throat chakra and helps with speaking abilities if worn as a necklace.

## TOURMALINE

Tourmaline is purity and positivity. It is a powerful crystal of great immediacy, quickly redirecting the energy of the mind and body. Tourmaline fights fearfulness and eliminates long-held wounds from the past, leaving you renewed and with far greater clarity. Whatever is weighing you down will soon be gone; your emotional baggage will be unpacked and lightened. Tourmaline is regarded as one of the best all-around healers. It is one of the most effective stones to use in overcoming a crisis or trauma and the accompanying pain. It relieves and releases sorrow and replaces it with joy. Tourmaline is also grounding, giving perspective regarding the very meaning of life.

The name apparently comes from the Sinhalese word *turamali,* the former name for "gems" in Sri Lanka. Tourmaline is found all over the world and comes in many colors, each one with distinctive properties.

+ **Blue** tourmaline, known as indicolite, is highly sought after. This stone relates to the upper torso and is healing for the brain, the pulmonary system, and the immune system. As with many blue crystals, tourmaline is superb for spiritual growth. It is a visionary stone and opens the third eye, giving way to psychism. This crystal enables you to see how you can serve humanity with higher mind awareness.

+ **Green** tourmaline, properly called chrome, is said to be the most powerful of all of the tourmalines, and a great many healers believe it is the most powerful of all crystals! Green tourmaline is healing to the eyes and heart and helps with weight loss. Anyone who suffers from chronic fatigue should try tourmaline. This stone also abets the study of herbalism. This crystal is a problem solver. It is a complete balancer, touching upon each chakra as well as rejuvenating the brain, the nervous system, and the immune system. Green tourmaline is a creativity crystal and lends enormous energy and impetus so you can strive for your best in work and art. Green tourmaline turns thoughts into actions, facilitating follow-through and helping you overcome any obstacle in your path. This is a confidence crystal, giving greater compassion, inspiration, prosperity, and tolerance for others.

+ **Purple** tourmaline is a stone of devotion. Lending the highest spiritual aspirations, this crystal works by connecting the root and the heart chakras. It greatly enables the ability to love unconditionally and creatively. Purple tourmaline is a heart healer.

+ **Black** tourmaline wards off negative energy and does not absorb it as most other black crystals do. If you sense that bad energy is being directed at you specifically and malevolently, black tourmaline will repel this psychic attack. Psychic vampires are also a problem, though they might be unconscious of it, but this crystal will keep them away and prevent them from draining you of energy. Black tourmaline is a guardian stone; keep it with you during times of stress. When held in the hand, black tourmaline relieves the symptoms of allergies within ten minutes. I would go so far as to suggest you keep it with you in your home, on your altar, and at your place of work, as it will make your personal space safe. This crystal shields against disease and strengthens the body. If nightmares or insomnia are any kind of issue, turn to tourmaline.

+ **Pink to red** tourmaline, called rubellite, is very soothing. This pretty crystal is an excellent one to use in a relationship that needs adjustment because it heals hurt and lends mutual understanding. Pink tourmaline can aid in overcoming inhibition in lovemaking; it provides trust in your own body and very gently allows you to let love in and to be able to receive love being shown to you. This is a stone of acceptance and release, paving the way to new experiences in love and in life. Pink tourmaline brings the most important kind of love of all—for yourself.

+ **Watermelon** tourmaline is an exceptional combination of green and pink and is a stone of harmony and balance. This crystal is one to call upon when dealing with conflict. It gives you the ability to love yourself and others, to understand, and to heal. It is a peacemaker's stone, more essential in this world than ever before.

+ **Clear** tourmaline is the blending of all the other tourmalines. This clear crystal touches upon and opens the crown chakra, creating synergy between the etheric body and the physical body by aligning the meridian lines. It is a boost to the immune system and has been used for healing nervous disorders.

## TURQUOISE

Here we have one of the oldest stones known to man. The Egyptians loved turquoise amulets and gifted them to their dead. The famous tomb of the pharaoh Tutankhamen was replete with turquoise, lapis, carnelian, and carved-stone talismanic figures such as scarabs. Egyptians were mining turquoise in 3200 B.C. in Sinai, and it has been held in the highest regard by many ancient peoples. The ancient Mexicans gave this stone the ultimate respect, using it only for the gods; it was never worn by mere mortals.

Turquoise is a copper-based stone, giving it the delightful blue-green coloring. The name comes from a word meaning "Turkish stone," as it first traveled to Europe along the Silk Route from Turkey. The black-veined specimens are called Navajo turquoise and are especially beloved for the grounding they provide. This stone opens the heart chakra and also affords a heart-centered quality, a loving connection with others. Turquoise releases negative emotions and draws out unsettling vibrations. If you use turquoise as a "drawing stone," I recommend that you place it on the ground afterward, because the earth can absorb and process the negativity that is no longer inside you.

Turquoise will help you find your deepest, truest self. It is a spirit stone that inspires and uplifts, literally offering elevation to the chakras. Turquoise tunes in to an individual's energy and projects it into the world. The stone gives gratitude and generosity and is a sign of friendship. Found all around the world, turquoise is revered in Native American and Asian traditions. These ancient cultures have had a belief that survives to this day that turquoise is a representation of the earth and sky.

The properties of this stone are as practical as they are spiritual—igniting intuition and enabling the wearer to grow toward wholeness. As a healer, turquoise can be placed gently upon an area of affliction for quick pain relief. It is especially helpful for headaches. Worn as a necklace, this stone touches upon the throat chakra, enabling eloquence in speech and encouraging absolute honesty. Turquoise is regarded as a planet-loving crystal, offering protection and preservation to the environment.

## UNAKITE

Unakite is a stone of vision. This mottled pink stone from South Africa helps you to connect with humanity on a mass scale through unconditional love. Unakite will heal wounds of separation and abandonment and can create balance between the physical and emotions.

Unakite helps you live in the present and get out of the past. It is a heart healer. Unakite aids the process of rebirthing and is also good for pregnant women—every kind of birthing. Here is a most wonderful aspect of unakite: It engenders self-love, which can attract and retain the love of others.

# VERY RARE ROCKS

### ATACAMITE—*Venusian Healer*

Atacamite is a rare green crystal from the Southern Hemisphere, specifically Australia, Chile, and Central America. As with other uncommon crystals, atacamite is only now being understood for its healing powers and is thought to be of great help to the genitals, thyroid gland, and nerves. Legend has it that it helps with "Venus diseases"—herpes and other STDs.

### AZURITE—*Jewel of Wisdom*

Azurite, found in the state of Arizona, is in the malachite family but is much less common. It takes its blue color from the copper contained within. Azurite was rumored to be the philosopher's stone and has an ancient reputation as an Egyptian jewel of wisdom, whereby priests and priestesses relied upon it for deepening spiritual awareness. The beautiful deep blue color is quite compelling and gave azurite wide favor with psychics throughout the ages, including the famed Edgar Cayce, who used it to hone his psychic power.

It seemed no praise was too great for azurite in times past, when it was reputed to restore the brain and help unborn babies form. Now, it is worn for letting go of the past and for accepting what is to come, while seeing deep within. Azurite is good for the skin and bones as well as the spleen and thyroid. This meditation stone is most helpful if worn as a ring on the right hand.

### BENITOITE—*California's Own Gem*

The more obscure stones are fascinating. According to the University of California, in Berkeley, California, benitoite is found *only* in California, but in

## Tips 'n' Tricks

### THE LIGHT OF LAPIS

In Egypt, a scarab carved from lapis lazuli was double the power of any other, as both the stone and the beetle represented infinity. Longevity and an illuminated mind come to the owner of a lapis scarab.

my research, I discovered that it has also been found in part of the American Southwest and in Belgium. I'm inclined to go with the word of the esteemed university's claim that is it a California-only gem; it has, in fact, been California's state gem since 1907. It was first discovered close to the headwaters of the San Benito River and comes in an array of shades of blue. At first, it was thought to be a form of sapphire due to the lovely, lustrous dark blue in the initial discovery. Interestingly, X-ray findings revealed that the internal structure of the crystal was unlike any other crystal on Earth. Benitoite is also fluorescent, issuing a pale blue glow under ultraviolet light.

This mysterious stone is linked to red-black neptunite, white natrolite, and yellow-brown joaquinite in that all these stones were formed in the cracks of serpentine rock under hydrothermal liquid containing iron, cesium, titanium, barium, and manganese. Specimens such as beautiful blue benitoite and red-black neptunite embedded in white natrolite are among the rarest on Earth and are found only in the part of California called the San Benito River valley.

With such a rare stone, much remains to be discovered about its properties, but a beneficial effect on the pituitary has been identified, and it is a stone useful to herbalists, botanists, and gardeners.

## BLUE LACE AGATE—*Earth Stone*

Ever since the famous photograph was taken from Apollo 8 in 1968 of Earth juxtaposed with the Moon, blue lace agate has gained an unprecedented popularity for its resemblance to Earth as seen from space. This stone is relatively new, discovered just forty years ago. Most agates are common, but the blue stones are rarer. Formed from liquefied silica and crocidolite, this stone gets its lace pattern from fractures and layers caused by centuries of heating and cooling. There is one great source for this pale blue treasure in Angus, Scotland, and it occurs rarely in North America.

This cool blue stone is a calming agent and can be used in meditation to achieve higher consciousness. It is believed to be able to open the third eye and therefore promote greater spirituality and attunement of the crown chakra as well as the throat and heart. It can also assist in disorders of the pancreas, capillaries, and nerves. In powdered form, in an elixir, it can help with hydrocephalus and other brain-fluid imbalances. Blue lace agate strengthens the bones, too, and can be worn to heal fractures and breaks more quickly and relieve symptoms of arthritis.

*Tips 'n' Tricks*

## CREATIVITY CRYSTALS

Two stones that benefit artists and musicians the most are amethyst and aquamarine; absorption of the color rays or vibrations of these crystals stimulates the centers of the cortex that create.

## BOJI STONE—*Millennium Mineral*

This mineral, so nicknamed because it gained popularity right before the millennium, is found in a small region of Kansas. A rare marcasite nodule, it is fragile and can crumble from overexposure to air.

## CHAROITE—*Russian Rarity*

It is a testimony to the earth that we are still discovering new crystals and gems. Charoite is a fairly recent discovery to the West, which became aware of its existence in 1978, although the Russians unearthed it in 1947 in the Chara River valley in Central Siberia. Indeed, the wavy patterning of this purple stone rather resembles a running river. Charoite is found exclusively in the part of Russia at the northern tip of Lake Baikal. Charoite is an intense purple. Since this is such a relatively recent discovery, we are still learning a lot about charoite, but what we know now is that it is a stone of cleansing and purification. It is also rapidly gaining a reputation as a stone of deep transformation. Charoite is being used for chakra healing, uniting the crown and heart chakras. An aura purifier, charoite grounds and integrates. It may be helpful for treating general aches and pains and issues relating to the heart, liver, eyes, and pancreas. This beautiful purple crystal can create the proper atmosphere for unconditional love. To use charoite effectively, you should place it over your heart.

## CHIASTOLITE—*Crusader's Stone*

Chiastolite is an exceptional variety of andalusite mined in China, Sri Lanka, and Brazil. What sets chiastolite apart are the dark-colored clay and carbonaceous inclusions in the stone, which are usually black or brown. These inclusions line up symmetrically and often take the form of a cross, garnering the name "crusader's stone." The black specimens are called iron crosses.

Chiastolite is a mineral that assists with the mental faculties—critical thinking and analytic abilities. It is greatly valued as a creativity stone and is held dear for the way it aids in combining originality with practical thinking. This crystal will take a notion and give you the impetus to make the dream real. As is fitting for a crusader's stone (think Knight Templar!), chiastolite will bring answers to mysteries. It is used by metaphysicians to support astral travel. It is also a symbol of transmutation, death, and rebirth; this is very much a stone of change. Healers believe it can reduce fever and even repair any material! This significant stone is held in immense regard, perhaps due to its cross marking, which makes it like no other rock in the world.

## CITRINE—*Cairngorm Quartz*

This is the orange or yellow kind of quartz and is actually rather rare in nature. The citrines you are seeing in the marketplace are quartzes that have been heated—low-grade amethysts or smoky quartzes cooked at high temperatures to make them more valuable in the jewelry stores. You can tell if you try by looking for the more reddish orange shades these faked citrines have. On the other hand, real citrine may have started its natural life as amethyst but then got heated by Mother Nature herself in seismic or volcanic activity. Ametrine, one of my absolute favorite stones, is half amethyst and half citrine.

True citrine is found in France, Brazil, Russia, the United Kingdom, and North America. Citrine is quite often mistaken for topaz, a gem higher in monetary value. There are dealers who have taken advantage of naive collectors and sold them citrine as topaz. Citrine's sisters in the quartz family are amethyst, the purple color; milky quartz, a cloudy white; rock crystal, the clear variety; rose quartz, a pretty pink; and smoky quartz, which ranges from gray to brown.

## DEEP DISCIPLINE

If you occasionally have trouble disciplining yourself or are a procrastinator, black tourmaline is the answer for you. This is the most helpful of all black stones and brings forth the inner strength to attend to anything. This stone will make you serious, self-controlled, and stable. Wear black tourmaline when you need staying power.

---

Citrine, also called cairngorm, is a birthstone for November and helps with stomachaches. It is a crystal that helps to heighten mental clarity and creativity, increase powers of concentration, and overcome a poor memory. Citrine is an aura protector, touching the chakra system and even helping to repair holes in the aura. It opens the sacral and solar plexus chakras and kindles the crown chakra. Citrine is especially wonderful if you wear it as a jewel in rings while you are working and handling your money.

You should keep a chunk of citrine in your place of work because it will allow you to be able to hear and accept constructive criticism. Tradesmen in India kept citrine in their shops and bazaars to attract money and abundance. An immediate feng-shui cure would be to place a cluster of citrine crystals in your wealth corner. Citrine is also terrific to have on hand in your home, as it is a cleanser of the environment as well as the etheric body. Citrine can help maintain equilibrium between the yin and yang energies—the female and male.

Citrine is quite simply an essential to have; it promotes calmness and brings out a feeling of well-being and happiness. Citrine makes anyone want to be more active and is a strong motivator. So, greater success, better health, and more money? Give me citrine anytime!

## CREEDITE—*Powers of Perception*

Here is a rare sulfate typically found within highly oxidized ore. Found in North America, especially Mexico, it is most often a white stone but can occasionally come in a cobalt-blue or purple color. It is loveliest in the rich purple and occurs in unusual crystal formations. Creedite is a body cleanser and detoxifier. It encourages self-expression and can give rise to self-understanding as well as a deepened power of perception of others.

## DATOLITE—*Dividing Lines*

Mineral collectors love datolite. The name comes from the Greek word *dateisthai,* which means "to divide." Datolite is a fairly fragile rock; the name is no doubt a reference to the fact that datolite crumbles very easily due to its composition of calcium boron silicate hydroxide. It occurs in green, yellow, or brown, and very rarely in orange, red, or gray. It was first discovered in the United States in 1806 in the Connecticut River valley but has since been found in Russia, Canada, Mexico, Norway, Africa, and Michigan. Datolite has a group of sister stones, including bakerite, hingganite, and gadolinite, that can sometimes be found in sheet form. Datolite is most commonly found as a large nodule and in extremely infrequent cases is a faceted crystal. Pink datolite has the sweet name "sugar stone."

## DIOPTASE—*Beauty and Balance*

Dioptase is a vitality stone that cleanses all the chakras, giving vigor to mind, body, and spirit. This beautiful emerald green mineral is usually found as crystals massed together in Iran, Namibia, Peru, Chile, Madagascar, Russia, and South Africa. While it is fairly unknown, it is one of the best healing stones of our time, emanating very calming energy. People have also been experimenting with it for pain relief and lowering high blood pressure. The latest discovery about dioptase is that it can be useful for cellular disorders and immune problems; it is said to activate the production of T cells. It also gives respite to those with Ménière's disease. Dioptase is a balancing stone for female and male energies, the yin and yang. Dioptase is one of those very rare stones that both calms and energizes at the same time, making energy dense, soothing mental stress, and alleviating migraines. A wonderful aspect of dioptase is that this stone triggers past-life recollection and also enables people to live in the present moment—two opposite and extremely positive occurrences. But my favorite aspect of dioptase is that it helps with matters of love. The stone heals a broken heart and opens it to higher love.

## LAZULITE—*Stone of Heaven*

Lazulite, coming from the Arabic word for heaven, got its name for the lovely sky blue color. It also occurs in a pretty oceanic blue or green. This is another one of those stones that has yet to hit major, mainstream popularity, but it might not happen because it is fairly obscure and rare. Lazulite can be found throughout North America and in the diverse locations of Brazil and Afghanistan. It is a calming crystal and offers clarity in health matters, as well, in that it is a filtering and cleansing agent of the blood and the immune system.

I predict lazulite *will* become enormously trendy as soon as people find out that it is a great stone for organizing. It seems that the feng shui, decluttering, and organizing bug has really taken hold in our current culture. So, help me spread the word—get your act together with lazulite! Lazulite clears away blocks and helps line ideas up in your mind, so you can then replicate them in your outer world. While lazulite is an aid to getting structured, it also prevents compulsive or addictive personality behaviors. It is great for stopping worry.

Meditating with lazulite will help you increase your sense of self-worth. This same crystalline quality can also keep obstacles from getting in the way of your creativity and communication. Personally, I feel like I need to encrust my walls with lazulite.

## LEPIDOLITE—*Letting-Go Stone*

Lepidolite should be called the letting-go stone. It's like a fresh breeze coming into a room filled with stale air. In elixir form, it is a wonderful way to deal with addictive behavior or to rid yourself of old patterns that no longer serve you or are potentially unhealthy. This uncommon mica, an ore of lithium, has only recently come onto the gem and mineral market. It is shiny and platelike in appearance, usually occurring in a pretty, pearly pink or purple color. On occasion, it appears white, and very rarely, it shows up in gray or yellow. This mineral occurs in Brazil, Russia, California, and a few spots throughout Africa. My favorite specimens are the single, large sheets of the lovely mica, which are called books and are an unforgettable violet.

Lepidolite is a great stone for getting a handle on anger issues. It soothes unresolved resentments, hatred, and frustrations. It is another mental stone and amplifies thoughts. Lepidolite is almost like a fairy stone in that it attracts positive energy, brightens spirits, and increases intuition. This is one powerful chakra healer, particularly for the heart and root chakras. One of the most important uses for this stone, albeit with great care, is for healing issues resulting from incest. Lepidolite is *so* powerful that you can even help manic depression and schizophrenia with it. While I usually have pleasant Piscean dreams, I had a bout with upsetting dreams and nightmares, and lepidolite came to my aid.

If you are lucky enough to come across a lepidolite that has fused with a rubellite tourmaline, then you have a rare rock indeed, and one that has double

## Tips 'n' Tricks

### LEPIDOLITE LUCK

One quick way to deal with negative and hard emotions is to place some lepidolite stones in a circle and light a pink candle in the center of the circle. Hold one lepidolite stone in your left hand and concentrate on what is holding you back, both spiritually and psychologically. With each issue, feeling, or concern, say, "I let go of _____." Picture the problem going into the stone in your left hand. When you are feeling full of calm energy, place the pink stone outside your house (where no one will pick it up) and know that you have rid your home, personal space, and psyche of these woes! Whenever you feel the need, let go with lepidolite!

---

the power of any other lepidolite. This mauve mica is a commanding tuner for the etheric body, raising the frequency, tone, and pitch of energy in your head. Chakra healers have reported that lepidolite sends energy in a gentle and profoundly medicinal way from the heart chakra to the crown chakra and back again, strengthening the "cord" attaching the etheric body to our body and soul, and to the here and now.

### SODALITE—*Truth-Teller's Stone*

Sodalite is a truth-teller's stone. When wearing it, you have no choice but to express what is in your heart and what you know to be real and right. It is a stone of sincerity. This blue crystal splendor is a relatively rare rock. There are only four known deposits of sodalite in the world: the town of Bancroft, Ontario, where it was first discovered in 1892, two other spots in Canada, and Maine. Sodalite, named for its high sodium content, is the result of volcanic activity in which nepheline rocks were flooded by sodium chlorine, giving this stone the unmatched royal blue color that makes for fine gems when cut. This may well be the reason sodalite is an environmental cleanser, reducing radioactive pollution.

Sodalite is also a balancer and aura cleanser. It is a simplifier, too, showing you how to reorganize your life and reduce stress and wasted time and energy. With this crystal, you will achieve the goals that are right for you on a spiritual level. It is a mental crystal that helps the synapses to fire smoothly and helps you retain wisdom. Sodalite impacts both hemispheres of the brain: the rational, linear half and the imaginative, intuitional side. This rare rock has the rare ability to give you great ideas as well as the impetus and planning ability to make them happen. Sodalite is good for people who are indecisive and easily confused. If you have to make an important decision, meditate with sodalite and you will arrive at exactly the right solution. Tremendous for communication, this stone is good for anyone doing public presentations. It provides the confidence and creativity to express yourself more freely and more honestly.

A popular carving stone, sodalite is also coming into vogue as jewelry. Healers use it for digestive issues and to work with diabetes. It is quite good as a massage tool in wand form or as a ball or egg that can be run over the body lightly. As an elixir, it gives confidence, helps lymphoma, and reduces inflammation. If you feel you're overbusy and that your life is just a little too complicated, wear sodalite at work. Clarity will come!

# Martian Moldavite

Here is a rock so rare, it is extraterrestrial! Moldavite is the only known gem-quality crystal that comes from outer space. About twenty million years ago, there was a meteor shower in the Czech Republic's Moldau Valley, leading to the only known occurrence of moldavite to this day. As a medieval scholar, I find the association with the legend of the Holy Grail and moldavite to be of utmost importance. For one, Excalibur, King Arthur's sacred sword, was supposedly forged from the iron of a meteorite. In Wolfram von Eschenbach's *Parzival*, the grail is a *lapsit exillis* (stone out of the heavens). Many other theories equate moldavite with the philosopher's stone, the long-sought source of wisdom for all alchemists, and it is even thought to perhaps be the sacred stone of Islam in Mecca, the center of the Muslim faith.

As such, moldavite is widely believed to be one of the stones that will help humans evolve. I had heard miraculous stories about moldavite that, quite frankly, I didn't believe until my friend Bill Cocke loaned me the book *Moldavite: Starborn Stone of Transformation,* by a couple, Robert Simmons and Kathy Warner. Upon reading this book, I grew so curious; I felt I *had* to get some moldavite. Kathy Warner wrote of her immediate spiritual connection and growth from the stone and how it helped her to trust in the universe enough to open a crystal shop, Heaven and Earth, in Gloucester, Massachusetts, with no money, no plan, a few rocks, and a lot of faith. I was also struck by the episodes in which the authors told of customers that came in, browsed around their shop, and often had incredible encounters with the bottle-green tektite. Kathy even named the physical reaction the moldavite flush. People sweated, turned red, and either laughed or cried. But what really made me curious was Robert's story of how he had had no reaction at all to the moldavite for many months and then, after patient meditation, he had a magnificent spiritual awakening. Robert's story appealed to the skeptic in me. What if I got some moldavite and it had no effect on me? Well, just in case, I could take comfort in Robert's long-delayed epiphany.

So, the same friend who alerted me to the moldavite went to the Psychic Eye in San Francisco, got a lovely green sliver, and brought it back to me while I was at work on this very book. I took it out of the bag and touched it, noticing how it felt rather like a piece of textured plastic. Bill looked at me with that charming grin of his and a twinkle in his eye and told me that he had gotten some moldavite for several of our friends. He seemed excited. Bill was a moldavite initiate, and just having it around had already made him happier. For himself, he had gotten a moldavite pendant, and he showed me how he could also wear it as a headband. I noticed that the moldavite rested on the exact spot of Bill's third eye. I didn't really feel anything except that it did rapidly pick up the heat from my hand, and seemed to hold it. Anyway, I felt rather disappointed that I didn't have a reaction like those I had read about in the book *Moldavite*. I was, after all, hoping to feel exhilarated and ecstatic. Who wouldn't?

The next day, I was to go to my own birthday party at a place in San Francisco's Chinatown called Li Po, named for the great drunken Chinese poet. Apart from being a bit grimy, the bar is a re-creation of a Buddhist shrine set in a cave with lanterns, incense, and many sacred icons, including some fabulous Buddhas. I was looking forward to my party but was also worried about the deadline on this book, feeling stressed, and, as always, more concerned about my friends' happiness than my own.

That morning, I woke up feeling a bit odd and couldn't go to the office to write. For four months, I had worked seven days a week; I had assigned myself a strict per-day word count, and if I didn't make my word minimum, I would beat myself up and increase the already considerable pressure on myself. I had planned to work all day and then go to the party. By midafternoon, I felt hot and uncomfortable. I tried to read but couldn't concentrate on anything. By the evening, I was in the midst of a full-fledged fever and was nearly delirious for two days straight. I missed several days of work and gave up any idea that I could work on this book. I simply had to give in to my body and let it all go. I heard the party was fun and everybody got along great. For me, an almost compulsively social person and overgiver, not attending my own birthday party was unthinkable. Interestingly, it happened, and there was no catastrophe. But, the big news was that I had put *my health* and myself first.

Afterward, I felt clear, and somehow lighter. Even though I was tragically far behind on all my various projects and duties, I wasn't worried. I knew they would get done in good time.

A thought had flickered through my feverish mind as I lay in bed unable to even lift the remote control to adjust the TV—could that have been the moldavite? It seemed like a silly idea, and I figured I had just caught a flu that came on very suddenly. I had left Robert and Kathy's book on my writing desk at my office and figured I would reread the moldavite encounters section to see if anyone had had similar reactions. Here is what I found as I paged through their book: "Also for many people, there seems to be a cleansing process involved. Here the moldavite energies go first where there are blockages. When these have been released, there usually follows a pleasant lightness of emotion."

I have gone on to read many stories of people who at first felt ill or felt like they opened a door into a new reality. Others quit jobs that made them miserable, got out of toxic relationships, moved across the country, and made many other fairly drastic changes. Whatever the change may be, moldavite *transforms* with no turning back and absolutely no doubt.

I have kept my moldavite crystal on my writing desk to accompany me during the transformative journey of writing this book. I plan to further explore the outer reaches of my moldavite revolution through meditation. I am ready to shed a lot of old habits, old possessions, old ideas, and old ways of being that no longer serve me. I want to grow in consciousness and cleanse my "doors of perception."

I urge you to do the same!

# CONCLUSION

You are now well on your way in the enchanted realm that is the world of gem magic. You know which stones will calm you, which crystals can cure you, and which rocks will bring you love and money. Your boss need never know that the lovely crystal specimen on your desk is one of the reasons you are his best employee. Your boyfriend can live without knowing the secret of your carnal carnelian necklace. Your fussy neighbor will never realize that you have kept her at bay with a jet obelisk in the window. All these little (and big) improvements in your life are now part of your unique set of trade secrets and tools for leading a charmed life.

Blessed be to you and yours!